How To Write A Historical Novel And Love It

~ A Beginner's Guide to Researching, Writing and Publishing a Historical Book

By TL Clark

Published in the United Kingdom by:

Steamy Kettle Publishing

First published in electronic format and in print in 2023.

Text copyright © 2023 TL Clark

All rights reserved. No portion of this book may be reproduced, stored in a retrieval system or transmitted at any time or by any means mechanical, electronic, photocopying, recording, or otherwise without prior written permission of the publisher.

The right of TL Clark to be identified as the author of this work has been asserted by her in accordance with the Copyright, Designs and Patents Act 1988.

ISBN: 978-0-9956117-7-1

To the best of the author's knowledge, all facts are correct at the time of publishing.

To the best of the author's knowledge, all facts are correct at the time of publishing.

Updated 2025 with minor amendments as some processes changed.

Acknowledgements

Cover design by RL Design
www.gobookcoverdesign.com

My gratitude to my husband, as always – my number one fan and the guy who ensures I'm fed and caffeinated even in my deepest writing state.

My editor, alpha, beater and proof readers have my undying appreciation.

And thank you, dear reader, for choosing this book. May it assist you on your exciting writing path.

Dedication

This book is dedicated to all brave souls who become writers/authors.
Maybe only other authors truly understand the courage it takes to put your work out there.
The struggles as much as the joys are all part of this crazy path.
I see you. I stand with you.

Table of Contents

Chapter	Page No.
RESEARCHING	
When?	1
What?	25
Why?	35
Where?	43
Who?	59
WRITING	
The Story Basics	97
Writing Tips	109
Formatting	119
PUBLISHING	
Publishing Options	131
Writing the Book Description	141
Reviews	147
Advertising	149
Checklist for Self-Publishing	157
Final Thoughts	159
Useful Websites	160
About the Author	162
Other Books by TL Clark	163

Important Introduction

I just want to say, right from the start...
THERE IS NO ONE WAY TO WRITE A BOOK.

My purpose here is to help you as best I can from my own perspective and experience.

Feel free to cherish some bits and disregard others as you please. My intention is to assist you in creating a historically accurate novel.

At the end of the day, you need to **write your book your way**.

This is an introductory level guide, intended for those embarking on their writing career.

I appreciate that not all historical novels adhere to the principle of authenticity. But this is a guide to achieving just that. And, as you've made the purchase, I'm going to assume you're interested in writing a historical novel with some degree of accuracy.

I've set the sections out into what my brain says is a logical order. Try reading it through first before applying your own order to your notes.

I am a proud pantser (make stories up as I go along). However, when diving into history, even I like to have some basics under my wing before forging my path into my first draft – forewarned is forearmed. It just makes writing a bit easier.

When I do my research, I have a Word document where I copy & paste notes (or write reminders from textbooks with citations) and include web links to helpful sites. You may want to do the same.

As someone who performs better with pictures, I also keep a storyboard on Pinterest and some images saved in my book's computer folder. My main characters also get an internet image applied to them.

We'll be dealing with the age-old questions, **"Who, what, why, where, when?"**, but not necessarily in that order. There will also be tips on formatting, editing and publishing – although, these will be high-level and are not intended as a comprehensive guide. There are many resources should you require further details in those areas.

I'll set a task at the end of each section to help get your little grey cells into gear. I was going to leave you blank spaces for notetaking, but I changed my mind; I'm giving you the perfect excuse to buy a fab notebook so you can make copious notes separately. After all, you may well go through this process for more than one novel.

By the end of this book, you should have a framework of what you're writing about; a story clothesline, if you will, upon which to hang the threads of your story. And a better idea of the publishing process.

In the back of this book, you will find some helpful websites to put you on your path to becoming a published author. Eep!

OK, enough pre-amble. Shall we get on with it? Alrighty, let's go travel through time…

RESEARCHING

When?

Alright, let's start with the basic questions to get your mind whirring. Don't be scared. I'm right here, guiding you through. One step at a time.

So, the question of when sounds like a simple one, right? You may be thinking, "I want to write a Victorian romance". Ah, but when specifically?

Or maybe you haven't even got that far yet. And now you're a bit confuddled. I'm going to take you through the general eras in a moment so you're crystal clear on which one you're drawn to.

Whichever time period you choose, it's always good to narrow it down to a year (or timeframe if you're writing about several years). You don't necessarily have to mention the date in your novel, but you need to at least know it in your head.

The reason for this is that even tiny changes can make huge differences. Look at 2020 – not too closely, it's depressing! But it's totally different from 2019. And so it is when we travel back through history. Ooh, tingles, we're going time travelling, folks!

Era

I've seen, in particular, a lot of confusion between the Georgian and Regency eras. I've even seen Regency books with the hashtag "medieval" – a few hundred years out there. So, this seems a good point to add in a 'history of Britain'.

If you're writing about other countries (or even your own, come to mention it), just be sure you know your timeline. I can't include everywhere, and as I'm a British author writing about British people, that's what you're getting as a main example.

Even this is not a definitive list; most ages can be split down into different eras, and there's always debate on such things, especially as we go further back. But I wanted to give you a general definition first. Think of the different times in terms of Chaucer, Shakespeare, Jane Austen, Charles Dickens, HG Wells and JRR Tolkien.

We all have very different life experiences. But some things never change. Together, we'll explore the possibilities. Try to leave behind pre-conceived notions of life through the ages. As you research, you will quite possibly uncover surprising facts – I want you to be open to these.

e.g. I had always assumed the Regency era was straight-laced, all prim and proper as Jane Austen portrayed it. But actually, there was an awful lot of debauchery and (*whispers*) many orgies!

And my initial thoughts of what a knight in my medieval romance should be like were quickly quashed. He changed from a jousting tournament, battling hero to more of a rural gent who was trained to fight and may be called upon to do so, but that was not his primary role. The knights of the 15th century were vastly different from their counterparts in the 5th and even 13th centuries – all considered medieval. But that period lasted so long that many changes took place.

So, my message here is; keep your mind open and be prepared to challenge your beliefs. Books and films have led us astray in some areas of historical knowledge. As have the Victorians – they rewrote a lot of history.

I'd also like to mention before we get really stuck in...if your characters talk to you, listen! Yes, I know it sounds totally crazy. But don't worry. Honestly, it's perfectly normal for authors to experience this. I was so glad when I found the writing community online and discovered I wasn't going mad. We spend so much time thinking about our characters that we can conjure them up in our mind's eye. A good film to watch which portrays this well is "The Man Who Invented Christmas" – it's about Charles Dickens and is entertaining as well as enlightening.

However, not everyone has that weird experience and that's OK too.

Some people are visual, and 'see' their books in their mind, like a movie. Others craft their stories more technically. There is no one right way, just what is right for you.

Types of Writer

Whilst I'm on a roll, there are *pantsers* who make the story up as they go along; flying by the seat of their pants. I'm in that category. I often liken my writing experience to channelling Reiki, it's just on a different frequency. My stories come to me in the place between sleep and awake. I sort of sit at my laptop, letting words drip from my fingers. It's exciting to see what happens – I discover as I write.

However, there are also *plotters*. Those who outline and plan their story meticulously before they write a single word of their manuscript. They create their plots, characters and worlds beforehand.

And there are even *plantsers* who do a little of both. They write a synopsis and plan key points, such as the inciting incident, dilemma and climax. Knowing what is going to happen is important to them. There will probably be many sticky notes in their writing area.

I guess the method outlined in this book falls under plantser really. By doing the research needed beforehand, we gather an idea of what our story will look like. Trust me, there will still be things you will need to look up as you go along. But at least you'll avoid having to interrupt your line of thought every five minutes by having some preparations in place.

So, getting back to it, I've started with the Neolithic period, but feel free to venture further back if the desire grabs you. The Stone Age could be fun to look at, but I'm assuming most of you reading this won't set a story that far back (note to self; explore this new niche – LOL).

By the way, and sorry to be 'this is how to suck eggs', but the century is named later than it sounds. So, the 1800s are in the 19th century. BC started year 0, effectively. We are living in the 21st century but our years start with a '20'.

OK, let's give you this list.

Historical Periods of Britain

ANCIENT BRITAIN

- ❖ Neolithic: c12,000 BC – c2,750 BC
- ❖ Bronze Age (& Beaker People): c2,750 BC – 750 BC
- ❖ Iron Age (& La Tène Culture): c750 BC – 43 AD
- ❖ Roman Britain: 43 AD – 410 AD

THE MIDDLE AGES (aka DARK AGES OR MEDIEVAL/MEDIAEVAL)

(~ splits into Early/Middle/Late Middle Ages)

- ❖ Dark Ages start: 410 AD
- ❖ Anglo-Saxon (raids & settlement) (fabled King Arthur lives here!): 449 – c550
- ❖ Separate Anglo-Saxon Kingdoms: c550 – 924
- ❖ United Anglo-Saxon: 924 – 1066

(Danish Rule: 1016 – 1042)

- ❖ Norman Period: 1066 – 1154

(The Anarchy: 1135 – 1148) – shh, we don't mention that!

- ❖ The Plantagenets (ends with The Wars of the Roses): 1154 – 1485

(the fictional Robin Hood would have lived around the beginning of the 13th century)

EARLY MODERN BRITAIN

- ❖ The Tudors: 1485 – 1603

(Included as Tudors but also separately; Elizabethan Era: 1558 – 1603)

- ❖ The Stuarts: 1603 – 1714

THE MODERN AGE
- Hanoverian Era: 1714 – 1901
(Splits down into...)
- The Georgians: 1714 – 1837
- (Regency Era - when Prince George was in charge as Prince Regent: 1811 – 1820)
- Victorian (steampunk authors take note): 1837 – 1901
- Edwardian: 1901 – 1910
- The Windsors (God save the king!): 1910 – current (not Saxe-Coburg, lalala!)

I'd also like to give you a quick rundown of USA eras too, just for balance. I feel mean if I don't. There are conflicting opinions, so this is a generalisation.

Historical Periods of the USA

- Early America (maybe from The Ice Age to Colonial) – Pre-European Contact
- Exploration and Colonization (Colonial): 1492 – 1763
- Revolutionary Era: 1763 – 1789
- Constitutional Era (Republic): 1789 – 1815

(1800 – 1860: Antebellum era)
- American Expansionism: 1816 – 1860

(1828 – 1860: Age of Jackson)
- Civil War: 1861 – 1865
- Reconstruction: 1865 – 1877
- The Gilded (Industrial) Age: 1876 – 1900

(1900-1914: Progressive Era)
- American Imperialism: 1890 – 1920
- Roaring Twenties: 1920 – 1929
- The Great Depression: 1929 – 1941
- World War 2: 1939 – 1945
- Postwar America: 1946-1960

(1945 – 1989: Cold War)
- New Frontier: 1960 – 1968

- ❖ Social Change: 1960 - 1975
- ❖ Political Conservatism – 1980s
- ❖ Information Age: 1989 – 2000
- ❖ New Millenium: 2000 – 2016
- ❖ Pandemic and Cultural Change: 2017 - Present

So, hopefully, that's given you an understanding of when each time period occurred. But to better understand the lives of your characters we need to look further than just the era's dates and title. It's a good start but doesn't give us that in-depth understanding yet.

What you have above, is essentially a record of the English monarchy listed by their 'house', and the political stages of American history.

If you are writing about Britain, do bear in mind it didn't exist until 1707. Queen Anne was the first monarch of The United Kingdom of Great Britain; yay a woman was our first joint ruler! Before that, we had kings and queens of England only (with other nations having their own). This distinction may sound obvious, but I want to ensure that you start off on the right foot.

And even before that, we had separate kingdoms. Who the first king of England was is subject to debate. Offa of Mercia and Egbert of Wessex ruled large parts following Roman rule (who themselves were here much longer than I appreciated at school by the way). But majority is not all.

I will forever think of Alfred the Great (born 849 AD) as the first king, but using the same approach as above, he was King of Wessex only. Sorry, Alfred.

Æthelstan is now commonly regarded as the first King of England from 927 (King of Anglo-Saxons from 924).

But if you want to get super sniffy, William I in 1066 brought in the Anglo-Norman era and could claim the honour of being our first king. I guess it depends on your own heritage and beliefs. Let's just declare King Æthelstan as the first and move on, for I digress.

The point is, that in Britain alone, we have a long lineage of monarchs. I'm not going to list them all - you'd get bored. And you may be writing about England, Scotland or somewhere entirely different. And this would be an exceedingly long, dull book if I listed every ruler ever.

So, take a moment to think about **who was in charge** in your novel's country and time. Even if your book doesn't focus on the ruler, their influence will be felt throughout the land. Here's where libraries and internet searches come into play. I'm helping you learn to research, not doing all the research for you. Although, I do have several blog posts sharing my plethora of Regency and 15th century research notes (links to these can be found at the end of this book), so if you're writing about those periods you're quids in.

There may also be religious and/or political leaders who control much of your nation's power or way of thinking. What edicts are in place from the Pope in Rome, for example?

Examples of World Leaders/Influencers

- ❖ Is Henry VIII on the throne – and which wife is he married to?
- ❖ Is Abraham Lincoln in presidency, guiding through civil war and abolishing slavery?
- ❖ Is Erik The Red establishing rule in Greenland?
- ❖ Is Julius Caesar about to get got in Rome?
- ❖ Has St Francis of Assisi created a new order of monks?
- ❖ Has John Wycliffe written the first bible in English and been executed for heresy?
- ❖ Is Napoleon Bonaparte fighting his way through Europe?
- ❖ Is Winston Churchill about to send men to fight on the beaches?
- ❖ Is Mahatma Gandhi non-violently seeking independence for India?
- ❖ Is Martin Luther King Jr. on the march?

Whichever leader is prevalent in your book's time and country, how do they affect people's daily lives?

~ Is there peace? Or political conflict? Even war?
~ Are any of your characters going to have to go off and do battle?
~ Are your people politically or religiously oppressed?
~ Are there any incidents of mass violence?
~ Maybe there are riots or civil unrest?
~ What is the poverty/rich ratio of the populace?
~ What is the prominent religion of the country? How does that influence the laws and behaviours of the people? Does your character subscribe to that?

NB Their beliefs may differ from your own!

~ What does the social status quo look like? And are the rules of society easily obeyed by your characters?

e.g. Henry VIII is widely considered a tyrant. He changed the nation's religion, supposedly in order to divorce his first wife so he could marry Anne Boleyn. The English Reformation was a brutal, bloody time. The repercussions were felt throughout the land. Many people (a suspected 57,000) were executed under his reign, many because of heresy and/or treason. What was originally a very Catholic country, with a king answerable to the Pope, suddenly became Protestant; Henry VIII pretty much nominated himself head of The Church of England and split from Rome. Ultimate power (*maniacal laugh*).

Or, more recently the global effects of World War II were felt in every corner. One main leader triggered a domino effect. Fear and turmoil erupted everywhere. Death knocked on every door. From Gallipoli in Turkey to the sacrifices of the Americans, the service of Australians and Indians etc., and of course, the terror which tore through Europeans.

It's not just wars and tyrants which affect our lives. Natural disasters can have a major impact. Our little blue planet is quite turbulent. Where would Dorothy have been without a cyclone, eh? OK, that one's fictional. Noah and his flood?

Examples of Natural Disasters

- ❖ OK. Let's start with a less scary one. There was an asteroid around 66 million years ago which may have caused the mass extermination of the dinosaurs (and other species).

Before I continue, let me reassure you that when I was researching my Cli-Fi romance, "Love Gaia", I discovered it was incredibly difficult to wipe out all humans in one fell swoop.

- ❖ So, we start getting more relevant. There was the eruption of Vesuvius in Italy, in 79AD. It is one of the deadliest volcanic eruptions in European history, claiming up to 16,000 lives. The towns of Pompeii, Herculaneum, Oplontis and Stabiae were buried under ash.
- ❖ In 1931, China was hit by the Yangtze-Huai River floods, which killed around 4,000,000.
- ❖ The (Bubonic) Plague, aka The Black Death, swept through Europe, North Africa and the Near East in the 14th century. Its death toll is approximated to be up to 200 million between 1346-1353. And that's after the Great Famine wiped out 30-60% of the European population and around about a third of those in the Middle East, between 1315-1317. This had a knock-on effect of speeding the demise of feudalism, at least in England, due to the labour shortage. There were subsequent outbreaks throughout the 14th-17th centuries. The last occurrence of it in England was 1665-1666 when it was dubbed the Great Plague of London.

- ❖ 1666 also saw The Great Fire of London (not strictly a natural disaster as it started in a bakery – who knew flour was so explosive??). But most of central London was left in ruins, including St Paul's Cathedral. It possibly maybe ended the Great Plague due to the destruction of unsanitary living quarters and their rats.
- ❖ In 1918-1920, after World War I, there was an outbreak of Spanish Flu which infected around 500 million people worldwide. Because, y'know, humans hadn't suffered enough already!?
- ❖ Ethiopia was struck by drought and famine in 1984. This news reached global attention and Band Aid was launched in a desperate attempt to offer relief to the crisis which is believed to have affected around 8 million, created 400,000 refugees, displaced another 2.5 million, and killed over 1 million people.
- ❖ I'm not going to dwell on our current pandemic which I have dubbed "That Which Shan't Be Named". But I do feel we are going through a transitional period. As of February 2022, its death toll stands at 6-23 million (*eyerolls at wild guesstimation*).

That's quite enough of all that doom and gloom, I think. You get the idea; nature can be deadly.

~ So, ask yourself, what's going on in your character's land
~ Is there a famine or drought?
~ Are there any other natural disasters/hazards - tornadoes, storms, floods, tsunamis, landslides, pandemics, wildfires, or earthquakes?

Key Events in History

Each time period is marked with events, for better or for worse.

History is nothing if not turbulent. I have already alluded to wars. It is forever brewing (*author of this book sighs*). However much I don't like violence, this is a good starting point. It shows what your characters may have been doing – is your heroine living in fear of invasion? Is your hero off fighting 'foreigners'? We'll come to the specific 'who' later, but we're starting to get a real impression of the setting for your characters now.

Jane Austen, who wrote during the time of the Napoleonic Wars, very carefully didn't write about them. It's my belief she was writing satire to amuse and distract the populace. But you still get glimpses via her characters' conversations or the odd mention of militia and soldiers.

Leo Tolstoy published "War and Peace" in 1865-69. The book starts in the Russian city of St Petersburg in 1805. Napoleon's War is a key feature in the story. The story is noted for its realism. It definitely does include details of the war, but also how it affected those left behind.

When writing my own book, "Regency Love", I discovered some fun key events which took place in 1814 which became the reason I narrowed down my year to that one. For instance, the Summer of Celebrations sounded rather fun; celebrating victory over Napoleon and the anniversary of Hanoverian rule with extravagant parties. I got to feature a hot air balloon ride; yay.

- But there are also other 'fun' things, such as the Industrial Revolution which, well, revolutionised life in Europe and the USA. Economies started to be dominated by industry and machine manufacturing. It started in Britain in the 18th century (about 1733), with the rest of the world following suit later. France became an industrial power by 1848, and Germany in 1870. The US rose in power through the 19th and 20th centuries. Whereas China and India underwent theirs in the 20th century. Iron and steel were utilised. Fuels and power changed to include coal, the steam engine, electricity, petroleum and the internal combustion engine. Factories sprang up. And travel as well as communication changed.

- The first steam engine was built in 1799 in England (and 1801 in the US). This made a huge difference to production and travel.

- Calendars have changed too. In 45 BC, the Italians, under Julius Caesar, created the Julian calendar. The year of 365 days was divided into twelve months, with every 4th year being a leap year. However, in 1582, Pope Gregory XIII decided this was too inaccurate and issued the Gregorian calendar which we still use today.

- Gunpowder was invented back in 800AD in China. However, it didn't reach the Middle East until 1240, India in 1258, and Europe in 1300.

- ❖ The signing of the Magna Carta by the English King John in 1215. It was a form of peace treaty which limited the powers of the monarchy – the king was now no longer above the law. The barons had got a bit fed up with his misrule and excessive taxation. It's been amended over the years, but there still remain three clauses which are upheld in British Law today – the ban on cruel and unusual punishments, trial by a jury of one's peers and that justice should not be sold or unnecessarily delayed.
- ❖ From 1271-1295, Marco Polo travelled from Italy to Asia, perhaps China.
- ❖ 1350-1600, Italy underwent The Renaissance, rediscovering classical knowledge which led to innovations in arts and culture.
- ❖ Johannes Gutenberg invented the movable-type printing press in Germany around 1440. It was later brought to England by William Caxton in about 1475. It brought in standardised English and opened up the world of literature. But it also reduced the power of the Church, which had dominion over knowledge until then as they were the only ones who could really read or write.

This dramatically changed the landscape of literacy and knowledge. It was an information revolution.

Please, I would like to take a moment here to hold a minute's silence to pay my respects to this marvellous machinery which changed the world (*bows head reverently*).

Fun fact – the printing press is the reason we still use the terms upper and lower case – the capital letters were in the higher (upper) case on the stand.

- ❖ The French Revolution occurred 1789-1799. That ended their monarchy with a beheading, and all got very messy.
- ❖ Between 1807-1888, the UK, US, Mexico and Brazil abolished the slave trade.
- ❖ The use of the electric telegraph spread between 1832-1840, thus improving communication.
- ❖ Last example; the Suffragette Movement started their fight to win votes for women in 1893. When they won in 1918, the common man (i.e. working class chaps) also were awarded the right to vote. So, in 1929, all British adults (over the age of 21) were allowed to vote.

I feel that's a good place to leave that list. The point being that there have been inventions and events which have changed our world.

~ What are the living conditions like for your characters?
~ Are there protests?
~ How do they communicate?
~ Where do they work?
~ Can they read or write?
~ Do they have democracy?
~ Have any recent discoveries changed their life?

What Time is It?

Well, we haven't always had clocks and watches. They are a very recent invention, really.

This can get a bit complicated, so I'll try to be pretty basic here. After all, you're probably not going to get too bogged down by hours. But let's look at the medieval era and before: For centuries, we followed **Canonical Hours** – which dictated prayer times. Terms for these changed over the years, but roughly speaking, these were:

- Matins/Night Office/Nocturns (a later portion of Vigil, from 3 am to dawn)
- Lauds (a later portion of Vigils from dawn)
- Prime (early morning, the first hour of daylight, added during the 12th century)
- Terce (third hour)
- Sext (sixth hour)
- Nones (ninth hour)
- Vespers (sunset)
- Compline (end of the day before retiring)

~ The three major hours were Matins, Lauds and Vespers.
~ The minor hours were Terce, Sext, None and Compline.
~ The length of hours varied according to the amount of light: they were not split into equal lengths/minutes.

e.g. in 12th century London, Matins (first light) was rung at: 2.30am at midsummer , 5am at the equinox, but 6.40am during midwinter.

Similarly, vespers (last light), was rung at: 7pm at midsummer, 5pm at the equinox, but 3pm during midwinter.

Church bells would be rung to call the (seven or eight) hours. This was strictly regulated; woe betide anyone who rang bells outside the rules! They were also rung for celebrations, coronations, curfews, festivals, funerals, market openings, Sunday functions and weddings.

The breviary was created; a liturgical book for praying the canonical hours.

They did not generally have clocks. Although, some towns were starting to get fancy astronomical clocks (oooh!).

i.e. They wouldn't ask their friends to come round to their place at two o'clock.

There were, of course, **sundials**. Apparently, some peasants even had them on the bottom of their shoes! They'd take their shoes off, face the sun and see where the shadow of the heel fell; clever! Sundials remained a stalwart of time-telling until the invention of watches, really. They are amazingly accurate, after all.

One could not actually declare time cost you money in the Middle Ages. Merchants were not able to charge fees on unpaid debt as that was akin to charging interest, which was illegal for most of the era. Time belonged to God!

In the 12th century, trade expeditions started to bring Islamic and Chinese **water clocks** to Europe.

However, it wasn't until the 14th century that **mechanical clocks,** measuring equal hours, started to appear. Although, the first recorded clock was built around 996 AD.

Hourglasses came into force during the 15th century, particularly on ships. And the first **pendulum clock** was invented in 1656. Followed by more accurate clocks with a second hand, and pocket watches 1675-1700.

Blaise Pascal is said to have tied his pocket watch to his wrist with a piece of string in the 17th century – the first wristwatch. He was also the mathematician who invented an early calculator.

So, be careful when your characters ask what time it is.

Also, as previously mentioned, the **Gregorian calendar** (which we go by) wasn't brought in until 1582. Before that, the Julian calendar was used.

In addition to all of the aforementioned, we start to think of the legal system. What laws are your characters governed by? There have been some intriguing ones e.g. Sumptuary Laws actually dictating your clothing according to class.

<u>Examples of Laws</u>

- ❖ **Sumptuary Laws.** England went through a series of these:

    e.g. 1363 - Knights with land worth 400 marks (i.e. £266 13s 4d) annually and their families: may dress at their will, except they may wear no weasel fur, ermine or clothing of precious stones other than the jewels in women's hair.

- ❖ 1483 - All persons in England except the royal family were forbidden to wear gold or purple silk.

    - Persons below a duke could not wear cloth of gold or tissue, and no one below a lord could wear plain cloth of gold.

- The servants of husbandry (peasants), were not allowed to wear any material which cost more than 2s for the broad yard (No other class appears to have had a price limitation, just fabric restrictions.)

- Each and every class had to pay a fine for disregarding these laws.

❖ Henry VIII is rumoured to have even introduced a beard tax for a while!

❖ In 1647, the Puritans managed to pass a ban on Christmas via Parliament. Yes, they cancelled Christmas – boo! This led to riots, rebellions and eventually civil war. Happily, Charles II came to the throne in 1660 and promptly re-instated the celebration – hurrah!

❖ Incidentally, Christmas was also banned in Massachusetts Bay Colony, America in 1659.

❖ The pioneers travelling across the plains of America in the 19th century, especially along The Oregon Trail had to come up with their own laws. Well-organised wagon trains drew up a constitution code. More violent crimes were punishable by whipping. Whilst the most serious, such as rape and murder, were punishable by hanging or firing squad. Trials were hastily convened on the spot. The priority was to keep the party moving along.

❖ During WWI, The Defence of the Realm Act (DORA) decreed it to be illegal to whistle for London taxis. Wouldn't want to cause a disturbance should anyone mistake it for an air raid siren! I do wonder who whistles like that, but hey, I didn't make the rule.

❖ In the 1950s, France introduced a law which allows someone to marry a dead person. This makes much more sense put into the context of WWI. If the living person can prove that the deceased intended to marry them, the President and Justice Minister may approve the request. A ceremony is actually conducted next to a photo or picture of the bereaved. This then opens up marital rights to the widow/widower. Still in use today.

There are all sorts of weird and wonderful laws which have been placed throughout history. As mere commoners, our duty is but to obey - even when they seem unreasonable. I could mention the recent face-covering mandate, but I don't want to get too controversial.

~ So, what laws do your characters have to live by?
~ What is the punishment for breaking the law?

I do also have to mention the **weather**. It varies a lot, I know. But there are interesting weather events and not just the big-scale natural disasters I mentioned earlier.

Charles Dickens still influences our Christmas cards to this day; they're adorned with snowy images thanks to a cold spell when he was writing. In fact, dependant on region, a lot of the UK doesn't get much snow at all.

Weather may literally be the difference between life and death for your characters. A bad summer would see mass starvation in many eras, no matter where you were in the world.
e.g. Ancient Egyptians were reliant on the annual flooding of The Nile.

Stepping back onto the Oregon Trail in the USA – well, your travelling party may get trapped by snow or landslides, thus meeting a grizzly end.

Looking at Regency London for a second; there was a Frost Fair when an elephant walked on the frozen River Thames – I kid you not. See; weather can be interesting.

~ Does your setting have varied seasons?
~ Do they get snow?
~ Or is it roasting hot?
~ How much rain can they expect?

WHEN - TASK

So, we're getting a good idea of the setting/backdrop for your novel. Like one of those historical portraits where the artist would paint the background in advance and then paint the people in during the sitting. Or a cartoon artist of yesteryear hand-painting beautiful scenery as the backdrop to animate characters upon.

We're thinking about the era and year, and adding in thoughts of leadership, morality, laws, key events, weather and living conditions.

~ Decide which era captivates you.
~ Look up who the ruler was and if there were any power changes/struggles.
~ See if there are any interesting events which intrigue you.
~ Select your year/s.
~ Think about which season/time of year it is.
~ How did they measure time?
~ Did any major weather activity occur?
~ Were there any natural disasters?
~ Basically, what perils lie in store? What could potentially kill your character/s?

What?

Now you know your 'When', it's time to dig into 'What'.

What type of book are you going to write?

"That's easy. I'm going to write a historical novel, that's why I bought this book," I hear you cry.

Ah, but do you start with historical fiction or romance as the initial starting point? Well, it rather depends on what emphasis you place on love in your book, really.

Yes, if love is the central point in your story and has a 'happily ever after' (HEA), then you're writing a romance>historical.

Historical Romance Book Examples

This is where you find books such as the Bridgerton series, books by Grace Burrowes or titles such as "The Night Circus". (*coughs*) Also, books such as "Regency Love" and "Love in the Roses" by TL Clark (*wink*).

Love, as I said, is the key theme. Whether it's a meet-cute, enemies to lovers or marriage, your main character is going to fall in love. And everything else is going to happen around that.

Quick note: if you write a romance without a HEA (happily ever after), or at least a happy for now, you'll find readers prefer that to be categorised as 'women's fiction' as opposed to 'romance'.

There is a 'Historical' option under women's fiction, but currently, it does not go any further than that i.e. you can't specify the time period.

Historical Fiction Book Examples

Whereas, Literature & Fiction> Historical Fiction, is where you will find books such as "Where the Crawdads Sing", "The Nightingale" and "The Rose Code".

This path leads you into "more serious literary fiction", if you'll pardon the term (it does make me wince). Books here tend to be grittier with an emphasis on realism.

Love may appear, but it's not where the main focus is.

~ So, are you writing a historical romance or historical fiction?

Of course, there are always crossovers, but I don't want to confuse you.

So, you've decided whether your book is going to be historical fiction or historical romance. But which category/genre does it fit into? This isn't necessarily as easy as it first appears.

Category

Technically, *the book **category** is a division into classification.* Think of it as a group that shares broad key elements e.g. fiction or non-fiction.

There are the **BISAC** (Book Industry Standards and Communications) subject codes, aka categories. An internet search should take you to the BISG (Book Industry Study Group) website, which lists all BISACs.

Do **not** use FIC000000 FICTION / General – it is too vague.
But **do** start with the FICTION heading and drill down from there.

BISAC Subject Code Examples:
- FIC027070 - FICTION/Romance/Historical/Regency
- FIC027180 - FICTION / Romance / Historical / Viking
- FIC049040 - FICTION / African American & Black / Historical
- FIC014020 - FICTION / Historical / Medieval
- FIC014050 - FICTION / Historical / World War II

If your book is aimed at young readers and teens (ages 12-17), you should have at least one YOUNG ADULT FICTION or YOUNG ADULT NONFICTION code.
e.g. YAF024140 - YOUNG ADULT FICTION / Historical / United States / Colonial & Revolutionary Periods

Hint: you will need to know which BISAC/s (up to three) you want when you publish a paperback. This handy code helps you show what your main themes are and ensures all authors/publishers have one point of reference for categorising their work. Book shops and libraries also then know which section to place your book in. So, be as accurate as possible.

Genre

Is the classification system which may change over time and further defines style/content.

Now, those are the classic definitions. Just putting it out there so hard-nosed literary people don't get upset.

In the real world, book listing sites will ask you to pick category/ies (they really mean genre, but hey, let's go with it).

Now, there are genres (categories), e.g. 'romance', and these lead into **'subgenres'** (or subcategories) e.g. historical and down further into Regency etc.

I personally (yet figuratively), hop around romance subgenres like a loved-up froggy. I have contemporary, historical, paranormal, suspense and women's fiction books in my portfolio. But they are all in the romance genre/category. This is not my recommendation by the way; it actually makes life difficult. However, my authory mission is to explore different types of love. I don't make life easy for myself! Be kind to yourself and try to stick to one main subgenre.

Anyway, my suggestion is to browse a book site, such as Amazon. What categories do they have? When you select each category (genre) in the sidebar, you can drill down quite some way e.g. Kindle Store/Kindle eBooks/Literature & Fiction/World Literature/British Literature/British Historical Literature – yes, that is one long pathway.

There are also sites such as Publisher Rocket which help you find the most competitive categories for online stores.

Sub-genres

If we look at the example of Kindle eBooks>Romance> **Historical Romance**, there are currently further options on Amazon (US) of:
- American
- Ancient World
- Medieval
- Regency
- Scottish
- Tudor
- Victorian

Oh yes, these differ on each country's Amazon page. Not something to worry about at this stage. We're just trying to pin down in general terms what your book is about.

You are then given options for Romantic Heroes:
- Alpha Males
- BBW
- Bikers
- Cowboys
- Criminals & Outlaws
- Doctors
- Firefighters
- Highlanders
- Pirates
- Royalty & Aristocrats
- Spies
- Vikings
- Wealthy

If you write an LGBTQ+ historical romance, Amazon (.com) currently lists these under their own classification of Kindle eBooks> LGBTQ+ eBooks> Romance:
- Bisexual Romance
- Gay Romance
- Lesbian Romance
- Transgender Romance

(with the same Romantic Heroes options)

But, if we look at the historical fiction path, Literature & Fiction> **Historical Fiction**, we get:
- African
- Ancient
- Asian
- Australian & Oceanian
- Biographical
- British
- Caribbean & Latin American
- Chinese
- Classics
- European
- Fantasy
- French
- German
- Irish
- Italian
- Japanese
- Medieval
- Middle Eastern
- Mystery, Thriller & Suspense
- Norse & Icelandic
- Regency

- Religious
- Renaissance
- Russian
- Scottish
- Short Stories
- United States
- Women's Fiction
- World War I
- World War II

This leads to time period options:
- Ancient
- Medieval
- Renaissance
- 16th Century
- 17th Century
- 18th Century
- 19th Century
- 20th Century
- 21st Century

It is important to note that these are subject to change. And that each Amazon site lists things differently, so it's worth checking the site you expect to sell the most copies in. For most people, the US is the biggest marketplace. But, for instance, I get a large proportion of UK sales too.

~ What subgenre are you going to write?

Now, we are really getting a clearer understanding of which bookshelf your book will sit on.

Knowing these options can also influence some parts of your book. You may want to utilise one of the romantic hero types. Or take advantage of a less densely saturated subgenre?

~ So, which century and time period are you writing about?
~ Looking at the above options, are there other things such as location or romantic hero, or even theme that can pinpoint your story further?

In the **top 100** of your category/ies, who are the best-selling authors? What do their books look like? What do they write about? Are there key points which have similarities? Have they set a reader expectation?

Although you want your book to stand out from the crowd, there are generalisations which are expected.

- A book set in either World War will probably involve soldiers, violence and separation from loved ones.
- A Regency setting attracts ideas of romance or seduction on the marriage mart.
- There are Victorian constraints (not just from the corsets).
- What's a Highland romance without a hunky guy in a kilt?

Later, in The Story Basics section, I will be taking you through some story tropes to help with these too.

Whether you are writing historical fiction or historical romance, there are key points to cover in the research, which is why this book includes both. You still need to know your stuff. Hopefully, by working through these chapters, that task will seem less daunting.

WHAT - TASK

So, what type of story are you writing?

~ Decide your BISAC code/s
~ Choose your main genre (category) and subgenre
~ Do your characters need to play a certain role to fit a subgenre option?

Why?

Shall we pause for a moment to explore your 'why'?
This can be asked in a couple of ways.

Firstly, why are you writing at all?

Not being rude, I promise. No accusations inferred. But you do need to know your own motivation.

If you are writing to make money – please reconsider. There are far easier ways to do that.

I'm only saying this to keep it real. I don't want anyone to have a nasty shock.

Writing is hard! Very few writers make a living from their royalties. Most authors have another job with which to pay their bills. Never underestimate the importance of a roof over your head.

I often liken it to ballet dancers. You can physically see the strain their bodies are under – ever seen their feet? They dedicate their lives to their art. And after all that hard work - blood, sweat and tears - do they get paid a lot? No. Sadly not. They do it because they love it. And the same should be true of writing. It is a vocation. A passion.

Write because you love it!

There is no such thing as overnight success. Even the greats had their struggles. Harry Potter was rejected by *twelve* publishers. Beatrix Potter had so many rejections she resorted to basically self-publishing. Louisa May Alcott was told to, "Stick to teaching". And even Agatha Christie took five years to get a publishing deal. Oh, last one… Stephen King's first book got *thirty* rejections!

OK, I didn't mean to lecture you at all. Just to make you aware of the difficulties. But if writing is your passion, little details like this won't deter you for a moment.

There will be times of incredible **self-doubt** – I don't know a single author who hasn't experienced this at some point. But the thing is to keep writing. My own coping mechanism of shoving chocolate (and sometimes wine in case of chocolate malfunction) into the mouth of my Self Doubt is perhaps not the healthiest, so I don't offer it as advice. Maybe find a healthy coping mechanism? I hear others highly recommend a walk in fresh air.

Similarly, impostor syndrome is often a stumbling block. I believe it was Theodore Roosevelt who said, "Comparison is the thief of joy." Bear this in mind. It is all too easy to look at the eloquence and/or perceived success of another writer and feel you are not good enough. Don't do that! You write your book your way. You are good enough. Again, those aforementioned greats had moments of impostor syndrome too.

Besides, there have been some truly dreadful books which have achieved incredible notoriety.

There will be someone who enjoys your book.

I would add that you should still read your preferred genre. One can get inspiration and enjoyment. Just don't get stuck in the, "I'll never write like that" mindset. You probably won't, and that's OK – you have your own style, babe. But never plagiarise – shouldn't need to be said, really, but a few folks out there have been guilty of it, so thought I'd just make mention.

But there's also another why…

Why are you writing about that time in history?

Now, that's an important point. Please note, "Because I find it interesting," is a perfectly acceptable answer.

But maybe you have "an axe to grind"? Some socio-political point. Fair dos. There are plenty of good causes to highlight.

Or is it because you've read other books in that time, and you've found something you wish was discussed but never has been? Great. Write the book you want to read.

To be honest, my 'why' of "Regency Love" was a combination of reasons. I love Jane Austen and that era, but I always felt the women were a bit hard done by. I wanted to give them the voice they were denied at the time. To really explore what a young lady may have truly felt and thought upon entering the marriage mart. Quite a challenge when I live some two hundred years later, but that didn't stop me.

For "Love in the Roses", I wanted to explore whether the Middle Ages were truly as bleak as they're made out to be, and if love could flourish in such an environment.

I'll confess that my very first book was written because I read a popular series and thought, somewhat arrogantly, "Even I can write better than this tripe!" Challenge accepted! People read and enjoyed my first book, and the second story came to me incessantly. And now I can't imagine ever stopping. Writing, to me, is as essential as breathing now. Being a writer is who I am. My stories demand to be set loose into the world.

I write about different types of love because I'm fascinated that the one word 'love' has so many meanings and different feelings attached to it. And, let's face it, I love love!

Inspiration can come from a variety of sources; books/films/adverts/songs/dreams – it matters not. Just trust in the story.

There are many possible answers to 'why' and some may be deeply personal. It's fine. Just know for yourself.

Possible Whys

- ❖ Writing can be therapeutic. Maybe you've had some bad experiences which you now wish to turn into positives by using them as inspiration. Maybe your character will have a similar experience, highlighting that particular issue. Educate and inform.
- ❖ Or, it can be the flipside of the coin – someone you know has undergone an experience, and by writing, you get to explore and hopefully come to understand what they went through.
- ❖ Maybe you're an explorer and want to uncover mysteries of the world.
- ❖ Because since time immemorial, there have been storytellers who unite peoples by telling tales. You just happen to be one of them.
- ❖ There's a sort of stress relief when you write.
- ❖ Because you want to leave part of yourself behind in this world after you've left it. This is your legacy. Be part of history.
- ❖ Writing can make us feel more alive; a heightened sense of things around us.
- ❖ Writing gives you an excuse to find a moment of peace, to secrete yourself away.

- Putting "pen to paper" may help you organise your thoughts and bring clarity. There are complex thoughts you want to sort through. Cathartic!
- Sometimes, we just want/need to express ourselves. To share our thoughts with the world.
- Perhaps you want to challenge your own views by having your character act in a way you would or could not. Do they have lesser or greater freedom than you to do so?
- Maybe you're bored? Hey, no judgement. There are certain times (*coughs*) such as being stuck in lockdown when you have time on your hands. You always wanted to write a story and now you're going to give it a go.
- Is your day job unfulfilling? Writing scratches an itch and brings relief to a neglected part of your soul.
- Or perhaps you've been repressed and now want to express yourself. Make your voice heard!
- Maybe you're a natural wordsmith and find creating stories fun. Good – it can be fun. Not everyone has to be a neurotic author.
- Because, having searched far and wide, you can't find the book you want to read. Write it!
- What if your book could make an impact? Really make a difference? Be an inspiration.

WHY - TASK

~ Discover your motivation for writing – have a really good think about it. Be honest with yourself.
~ And think about the 'why' of your chosen era – are you up for the challenge?

Where?

The world is your oyster. You can select absolutely anywhere you want.

To be honest, you don't even have to restrict it to planet Earth, but then we're straying away from the historical context this 'how to' book is investigating. Although, I hear there are fantasy historicals – just saying.

Thanks to things such as Google Maps, one does not even have to have visited the place we write about. Although, it's essential to have a good understanding and knowledge of the location.

Historical Landmarks

There may be landmarks which you want to include.

~ Has the Eiffel Tower been built?
~ Is the Elizabeth Tower, housing Big Ben keeping watch over London?
~ Are the Egyptian pyramids looming large?
~ Is the Statue of Liberty standing guard over New York?
~ Are fun times being had in the Palace of Versailles?
~ Does your character see the Parthenon?
~ Maybe the Colosseum is used/seen?
~ Or do they walk the Great Wall of China?

Of course, they don't even need to be as grand as any of those. Your chosen town or village may well have its own historical landmark. Have a look.
e.g. Is there a particular church/cathedral in your character's hometown?

Alternatively, you can make places up. This is especially useful if something bad is going to happen and you have no desire to besmirch the good name of a real town. I tend to give new names but use real places as inspiration. Not always, but often.

Town vs Country

<u>Towns/Cities</u> – built up, busy, over-crowded, dirty (either from modern car pollution or horses and humans), hubs of commerce.

By the way, in the UK, city status may be given by the monarch, usually (but not necessarily) associated with a place having a cathedral (and/or, these days, a university). There are currently 69 cities in the UK.

<u>Countryside</u> – agriculture plays a vital role, so is busy in a very different way.

For most of human history, the vast majority of folk would have been involved in one way or another in agriculture. The time before supermarkets was one of homegrown produce. People would live in settlements, each supporting one another even indirectly e.g. tools supplied by the blacksmith were used in farming.

Although the percentage remained high in the rest of Europe, this declined in England around 1700, dropping to 40% from around 60% of the labour force working in agriculture. It's only in very recent times, from around the late 20th century this has been in steep decline. In 2019, only 1% of Brits worked the land. This is a global trend.

Now, there are more cities in Britain other than just London – this may come as a shock, LOL. The Georgians were very fond of Bath. Oddly, Bath was falling out of favour with the Regency folk, but it still gets mentioned in the genre fiction fairly often. London was, of course, a main draw for the Ton of the Regency era. And has been the focal point for many a historical event. But do consider other cities and towns.

Ireland, Wales and Scotland form our isles, and are equally important nations, by the way.

Examples of Historic Towns and Cities

- ❖ Athens, Greece has been standing for quite some time. Since 5,000 BC.
- ❖ Damascus, Syria is one of the oldest cities in the Middle East, with origins back to the 3rd millennium BC.
- ❖ Jericho in the Palestinian Territories is believed to be the oldest city in the world.
- ❖ St Augustine in Florida, USA boasts of being the country's oldest city. It was founded in 1565.
- ❖ Tende, France was founded in the 7th century, but prehistoric rock engravings have been found there.
- ❖ Bardejov, Slovakia still has houses built in the 13th to 15th centuries.

~ Which country is your book set in?
~ Is it in the town or countryside?
~ What does it look and smell like?
~ What are the streets like?
~ Are there key features or landmarks?

Distances

This is definitely worth a mention at this point. The UK still uses miles and has done for many many years. No kilometres, please; we're British! Ensure that if you refer to it, you use the appropriate measurement for your chosen country.

There are often old maps to be found online, which will help with getting your bearings.

And how did they get between destinations? Did your characters **travel**?

In Regency England, they had improved roads thanks to turnpikes and tolls. So, their horses and carriages were faster. As a rule of thumb, I looked at the old roads still in use and calculated the time it would take to cycle between points A and B. The speed was roughly 8-12mph for carriages, so gives a good, rough comparison.

Whereas back in the 15th century, the speed was more akin to walking pace and they didn't *really* use carriages. They had carts for belongings or covered wagons or litters (a sort of box supported by two poles, carried between two horses) for the elderly or infirm. Horse riding was the staple transport. And there is evidence to suggest ladies rode astride then!

And if you really want to get into detail, you may want to look up the breeds/types of horses your character could ride.

Horse Types of Medieval England

- Rouncey – an everyday, all-purpose horse
- Palfrey – slightly finer, used by knights and ladies. Good at trotting. Smoother gait.
- Lyard (dapple grey) – on par with a palfrey
- Courser – fast and strong, used by knights
- Destrier – elite and rare. Used in jousts and battles. Lower endurance.

The term workhorse covers pack horses/sumpters and cart horses. They were shorter and stockier. In fact, all horses were shorter than we know them today – closer to pony size by our standards.

The saddles had a high back and front, with a cantle which wrapped around the rider. Great for comfort and security…until the horse fell and you were trapped on, or needed to twist or jump over obstacles. Oops! Injuries and deaths were caused.

Side saddles really only emerged in England during the 16th century.

Whereas, your focus during the Regency era may shift to:

Types of Carriages

- Dog cart – single driver (room for dogs)
- Governess/Jaunting Cart – ladies or children would use these. Could be pulled by horse or donkey.
- Gig – really made for one person
- Curricle – sportster of its day; two-wheeled, fast, dangerous, pulled by a pair
- Phaeton – two-seater with four wheels (quite showy-offy)
- Hackney – think of it as a horsey London cab
- Post-chaise – intended for the post, but could carry two to four passengers
- Landau – similar to a barouche. Could be pulled by a pair or a team.
- Barouche – four-passenger, pulled by a team of four (or six). Convertible. Very grand.
- Family coach – enclosed, carrying four passengers, but unsuitable for long journeys

- ❖ Brake – could carry up to six sportsmen and their dogs to a hunting ground
- ❖ Stagecoach/Mailcoach – combined post and up to seven passengers and set up in relays/stages.

NB Before the car, there was probably horse poo to traverse wherever your characters find themselves.

Cars became widely available in the 20th century. But there were steam-propelled wheeled vehicles invented in the 18th century.

Barges were sometimes used. And, when canals were introduced, the transportation of goods became far easier.

The first steam locomotive (train) was invented in 1784, with the first working model made in 1804. The locomotive was built in 1825, which is when trains started coming into public use. The US got their first one in the 1830s.

Following on from freer transport, merchants rose as a class more and more. Commerce slowly became global. In medieval England, one could live or die by a good harvest. But, as imports increased, we gradually became less reliant on our own crops as our main food source.

~ How far are your towns, cities and/or villages from one another?
~ Do your characters have to travel?
~ If so, by what means? And how long does it take?
~ Are there toll roads?
~ Are there bandits along the route?

Communication

Along with transport comes information exchange. Emails and telephones are pretty new (do stop rolling your eyes; I know you know). But letter-writing wasn't even as quick as it is now. The postage stamp is a relatively new invention.

~ Did the person receiving the letter (or their servant) have to pay to get their mitts on it?

How long did the mail take to arrive? This sped up with improved road systems, telegrams, and better ships for overseas correspondence. My own Lady Anne had to wait an insufferably long time to send and receive word to a long-distance friend whom she had concerns for – around two months.

Back in medieval times, only clerics could really write, so households employed a scribe/clerk to read and write for them. And that was often in Latin. Oh, the power! Isabel in my medieval romance is lucky – she just about manages to come in at the right stage to be able to read and write herself.

I'll briefly mention **newspapers**. The first one published in Britain was in 1665 but was available to subscribers only and was a government press. 1712 was arguably when the first newspaper as we know it was issued.

In 1693, *The Ladies Mercury* was published as a form of monthly women's magazine (periodical) and it even had a sort of advice column answering correspondence. *The Gentleman's Magazine* wasn't published until 1731. I venture no inference on this. Alright, maybe a mild yay is permissible.

Before all this, there were people who travelled and spread news by word-of-mouth. In the late 15th century, friars were very popular dinner guests of ladies, for they had gossip to divulge.

Books

Books themselves were a form of communication. "The Canterbury Tales" by Geoffrey Chaucer is considered one of the most important books in history. Dating back to the late 14th century, it was one of the first to be written in Middle English and not French, and provides a tongue-in-cheek view of medieval life.

"Robinson Crusoe" by Daniel Defoe, published in 1719 is considered one of the first novels, depicting the extraordinary fictional life of an ordinary character.

In 1740, Samuel Richardson's moralistic "Pamela" helped bring the romantic novel into the mainstream.

In the mid-18th century, Britain had circulating libraries which were used via a subscription. These allowed more books to reach the hands of more readers, who couldn't necessarily afford to purchase a book.

However, it was also in the late 18th to early 19th centuries when young ladies were strongly discouraged from reading romantic novels as they may corrupt their delicate minds and lay them open to seduction (*gasp*).

~ Does your character read books?
~ Have they given them grandiose ideas?

~ How do your characters communicate?
~ Has the telephone been invented yet? Are your characters rich enough to own one if so?
~ Perhaps the telegraph is in use?
~ Do they have regular written correspondence?
~ How long does it take for a letter to arrive?
~ Are there speedy messenger services?

Language

Now, your 'where' will affect many things, including language. Ever tried reading Thomas Hardy? A very different **dialect** was used as it's set in rural historical England. I don't recommend going that heavy with language. I mean, books like Trainspotting are incredibly popular, but can also be difficult to understand. *But* you will want to bear dialect in mind. And maybe add a flavour or hint of it.

Incidentally, before the printing press standardised **Early Modern English** around 1500, there were different languages/dialects in use, such as West Midland, East Midland, Southern (including Kentish) and Northern. It was entirely possible for people from different parts of England not to understand one another.

The shift from Middle English saw a change in vowel sounds and our pronouns became gender-neutral. Our own Modern English is largely based on that of the East Midlands.

In literary terms, it's a shift from Chaucer to Shakespeare.

My own aim is to write sympathetically to the time period. Writing my medieval romance, it would've been imprudent to attempt to write in Early Modern English. I would've found it incredibly challenging to write and very few readers would be able to easily understand it. However, I tried very hard not to use modern jargon and have used time-appropriate words and phrasing, such as, "prythee" (a polite please). That changed spelling to "prithee" around 1560 by the way.

I wrote a hint of the old style of speaking. Speech patterns and phrasing were utilised.

If you do an internet search for the **etymology** of words, you'll find when their first recorded use was. Now, bear in mind, recorded use refers to written occurrence, and it's reasonable to suspect that the word was in oral use a little while before, except in cases such as Shakespeare who seemingly made up words, bless him.

Obviously, you don't want to do this for every single word. But it's great for keywords and phrases. A little sprinkling of cant is amusing, but don't overdo it.

My paranormal romance "Love Bites" is set in Wales. It pleased me to include a 'cwtch' – this is the most comforting type of hug you can have. I made sure to explain that in the text.

It can be fun to find old words to fling as **insults**. Swearing has changed a lot over the years – words which are innocuous now were once cause for fisticuffs or even suing. Yes, in Medieval England, a woman could sue another for being called a whore. Men thought it the most heinous insult in the world to be called a fool and could come to blows if thus affronted.

'A turd in your teeth' was a common insult back in the 15th century - it's so awesome I had to include it in my book. Along with words such as 'babblement', meaning foolish talk, and 'dalcop' which translates to dull-headed. 'Fopdoodle' is perhaps my favourite medieval insult, again meaning a stupid person. And yes, I included a lengthy glossary to provide meanings for words and terms no longer in common use.

Don't be afraid to use the thesaurus, often built into software such as Word. And a quick search for synonyms online can often lead the way to better words which may be more appropriate for your character/s.

Speaking of language; the rule of thumb is to use the spelling of the country your book is set in. The UK has weirdly different spelling and dialect from our American cousins. And the Canadians sort of mix the two together. We embrace these differences with love, of course. However, it can be jarring when reading if you have an English person walking along a sidewalk instead of a pavement. Or if your American character is eating crisps instead of chips. So many nuances to be mindful of!

e.g. I once had a reader question whether I meant a character *ate* tea – yes, because they were in northern England where tea can also mean dinner/evening meal. Well, actually, tea/dinner/supper usage varies wildly depending on region. Don't get me started on that path – it's a long, contentious, and complicated one. We drink tea. But we can also eat it too – it just changes meaning.

~ What language does your character speak?
~ Are there any localised words of dialect you'd like to include?
~ How do they swear?
~ Do they insult one another?
~ Can you write it in a way modern readers understand whilst giving the impression of their speech?

A Quick Note on Wildlife

Wildlife is different. Don't groan and roll your eyes. I've seen chipmunks mentioned in a UK setting (grr!). **NB** Highly unlikely to happen unless it escaped from a zoo. Please do check which creatures are roaming your chosen land/s if you refer to them.

- ❖ Does your character see/hunt deer?
- ❖ What birds are there? Are they hunters or prey?
- ❖ Do hedgehogs snuffle around at night?
- ❖ Do owls hoot? And are they good or bad omens?
- ❖ Speaking of screeching, ever heard foxes mating?
- ❖ Do wolves roam the land?
- ❖ Are crocodiles or alligators yet another threat?
- ❖ Do sharks or jellyfish swim in the local sea?
- ❖ Is there a majestic tiger stalking nearby?
- ❖ And are there any eerie sounds of critters in the night, keeping your character awake?

In summary, the entire globe has an incredibly rich history. But everywhere has its quiet and busy zones. Rome, Italy was a thriving hub (still is), but the outlying Italian towns and villages were also important. Pompeii wasn't in Rome, yet most people have heard of the volcano, Vesuvius, erupting in its catastrophic way.

The ancient Egyptians and Greeks are ever so fascinating. Africa, India, Scandinavia... a rich tapestry awaits wherever you land.

WHERE - TASK

Location is being narrowed down. And therefore, many aspects of life are affected.

~ Decide which country your story is set in.
~ Is the main focus on town or country?
~ Place your characters in a town/city/village – give it a name.
~ What does it look and smell like?
~ What landmarks are there?
~ What do your characters sound like (dialect/language)? Do they speak the same dialect?
~ What transportation did they use?
~ Is agriculture or trade more important in their economy?
~ Are there any critters around?
~ How did they send/receive news?

Who?

We finally come to the who. By now, you should have a good idea of the country, location and time period.

So, who are your main characters? You should really have only one main hero (protagonist) in your novel.

What is Your Character's Name?

If you look up the meaning of any of my main characters' names, you will discover a clue as to their role or personality. But you don't have to be as geeky as that, obviously. That's just a me thing.

However, their name should be time appropriate. Which names were most popular then? You didn't get many people named Britney or Brad until recently.

There are lots of lists online. If you ask The Internet which names were most popular in any given year or time period for a particular country, you'll find the answers you seek.

Examples of Popular British Names

In the medieval era, popular boys' names included:
- William
- John
- Richard
- Robert
- Henry

And the girls' top 5 were:
- Alice
- Matilda
- Agnes
- Margaret
- Joan

But in Regency England, you had:
- William (still at the top for boys)
- John
- Thomas (*snickers at that name sequence*)
- James
- George

The girls' names most in favour were:
- Mary
- Ann(e)
- Elizabeth
- Sarah
- Jane

Popular Names in 20th century France

Boys:
- Jean
- Louis
- Pierre
- Joseph
- Henri

Girls:
- Marie
- Jeanne
- Marguerite
- Germaine
- Louise

I'm not going to list every possibility, obviously. I just wanted to give you an idea of the variances in country and time. Clearly, you can go outside the most popular names, just bear in mind what was realistic for them.

Many authors report that their characters tell them their names. Largely, mine do, but I do the name-check thing still.

Another note on names – try to avoid ones which sound too similar to one another as it gets easily confusing for readers. And it's fine to have a supporting cast, but don't have too many, as again, it causes confusion.

I find it helpful to have a document where I have a picture of what I think characters look like, along with key attributes.

I also keep a spreadsheet (spot the ex-administrator!), to track character names (& meanings) and appearance (such as hair and eye colour) so they don't all end up named and/or looking the same. After eleven books, I'm very glad I have this.

~ What is your MC's name?
~ Check popular names from your chosen time.
~ Are they named after a family member or prominent person?

What Do Your Characters Look Like?

Don't forget to describe them. Rule of thumb – if you give any character a name you should give them some characteristics, so your readers know what they look like.

Are They Rich or Poor?

This will affect so many aspects of their life; motivation, employment, health, diet, clothing etc.

~ Ask yourself; how much do you want to make your character suffer?
~ Do they have aspirations?
~ Or are they stuck in their social sphere?

Fashion

I have heard it said and find it useful to think of fashions changing with each new monarch/leader. It's a good rule of thumb but isn't always the case.

Fashion is such a broad title and can change between regions, let alone countries. For example, I live in what is generally considered the countryside. When I go to London, I feel like a country bumpkin (less sophisticated) as my clothes and manners are slightly different.

In terms of fashion, one could start with the basics such as undergarments (*blushes*). Historians recently got excited when they found some rudimentary knickers and a bra which date back to the 15th century. Although, it's generally believed that Regency ladies didn't have knickers, so who knows what happened in the interim.

Petticoats

~ Does your leading lady have many layers of petticoats, a rounded farthingale (akin to Elizabeth I's), a wide pannier (like Marie Antoinette wore) a hooped crinoline (think Gone With The Wind), or a bustle which gave one the appearance of a bigger bum (late 19th century)?

~ Or maybe your lady wears a simpler kirtle/cotehardie (a laced-up garment over a smock/chemise but under the outer gown/surcoat)?

~ Does your man wear hose, pantaloons or trousers? Maybe a houppelande – long or short? How much leg was on show? Note that calf padding etc. was worn during some periods to add shapely definition.

Hats are fantastic in their variety.
~ The tall stovepipe (as worn by Abraham Lincoln), Moroccan fez, Russian furry ushanka, conical Asian hat or the bowler. And that's just the men!
~ Ladies have worn simple mop caps, crespine (hair netting), bonnets or berets.

Far too much variety to pinpoint every option. But headwear can be fun and give clues as to the character's role in society.

Head coverings/hats were still worn in the UK until recently, so ensure appropriate headwear is in situ.

Hair
Yes, even hair length comes and goes with fashion. Ever hear the term "highbrow", meaning posh? It comes from the medieval era when women would shave/pluck the hair from their forehead to make their hairline higher. Given the rest of their hair was tucked under head coverings, I surmise bald was considered a good look – LOL.

But if we travel to the roaring twenties, some ladies had very short hair.

And, again, men have their own trends too. The hippies of the 1970s were often told to, "Get a haircut!". Beards and moustaches, likewise, go through fads.

Of course, religious views often play their part in how/when we show our hair. Even now, a lot of religious buildings ask for head coverings before you enter.

Shoes
From the Middle Ages to the early 20th century, Europeans wore patten shoes. These were worn over a normal shoe when people went outside. The raised platform helped keep one's hemline out of all the detritus on the street.

I find the poulaine/Cracow fascinating; a leather shoe worn from the 14th-16th centuries. They had long, pointy toes which could reach up to 45cm. The church began to accuse these of encouraging sexual proclivity and sodomy! But at the same time, said they prevented people from kneeling (to pray), so…!? (*eyerolls, sighs*). In 1362, Pope Urban V banned them, and England restricted their length in sumptuary laws.

And for decency's sake, let us not show an ankle if it is not socially acceptable (*gasp*).

Colour
Colours have long had associations. We're all familiar with red means danger, I think. But what other meanings do they have?

Well, at least in the Middle Ages:
- Green stood for love
- Grey for sorrow
- Yellow for hostility
- Blue, partly because of its connection with the Virgin Mary, became the colour of fidelity.

Fun fact – orange wasn't truly used to name a colour until the 16th century when the fruit arrived in Europe. Before that, it only referred to the tree on which the fruit grew. William Shakespeare used the word in both contexts, but I don't think he was the first in all fairness. But anyway, that is why we have birds named robin redbreasts – their chests are actually orange, but when they were named, the colour orange wasn't in use.

Of course, some didn't have much of a choice in clothing. Servants of the 'inner house' (indoor staff) were given a **livery**. The term livery initially meant the whole pay package, including any allowance. Within this, clothing, or at least material for such, was given by the master of the house. A combination of colours of cloth, along with a "device" or badge to sew on, denoted which lord you served. The wearing of a livery only truly stopped when the hiring of servants such as footmen fell by the wayside i.e. after World War I. However, the royal courts of Europe still have livery for their servants for formal occasions.

~ Does your character have long or short hair? Is it hidden under a cap/hat?
~ What clothing do they have on?
~ What eye colour do they have?
~ Are beards in fashion for the men folk?
~ What is their complexion like? Is it pale from being indoors or rough and reddened by all the work they do outside?

Structure of Society

There is a long list of **peerage titles**, dependent on when and where you're writing about. I'm going to give an example here, but it only applies to the Regency era in Britain, so please use with caution. It's a good starting guide, at least.

Also, *how* you address people depends on the formality and whether it is in writing or speech, and time period.

Regency England Society Titles

Royalty – upper class – Referred to as "Your Highness"
- King – wife is a queen
- Prince/Princess

Members of the Peerage (allowed a seat in the House of Lords) – **nobility**
- Duke – referred to as Duke of (title) or Your Grace – wife is Duchess of (title)
- Marquess – referred to as The Marquess of (title) or Lord (title) – wife is a marchioness, Lady…(title)

The following are referred to as "Lord and Lady (title)"
- Earl – wife is a countess
- Viscount – wife is a viscountess
- Baron – wife is a baroness

Gentry (commoners; not nobles) – Second class
Addressed as Sir (first name) and Lady (surname)
- ❖ Baronet (hereditary, non-peer)
- ❖ Knight

Addressed as Mr. and Mrs.
- ❖ Landed squire / Esquire
- ❖ Gentleman

Labourers - Third class
- ❖ Doctors
- ❖ Bankers
- ❖ Clergy

Fourth class
- ❖ Lawyers
- ❖ Teachers
- ❖ Shipowners
- ❖ Artists
- ❖ Builders

It is worth noting the rarity of dukes. I know Regency novels go crazy over them. But they're basically sub-royalty (and quite probably related to the monarch). I included a couple in my own book, to be honest. But, in reality, there were only about 30 dukes in Regency England. Whereas there were around 140 earls and 120 barons.

Wealth

So, whether they were rich or poor, your character still needs a certain amount of money in order to live. But what were their living expenses and wages like? And what coins did they use?

My knowledge covers the British system, so that is what I'm using as examples. In all fairness, a lot of historical fiction is set in the UK, so I'm not being too mean.

Let me start by explaining **l, s, d** – no, not that kind. I'm talking **pounds, shillings and pence**. These abbreviations come from the Latin; liber, solidus and the Roman denarius.

15th Century England Coinage

- Groat
- Half groat
- Half penny
- Farthing

The pound wasn't an actual coin but was referenced for accounting. It was the equivalent of 240 pence or 20 shillings. The mark was 162 pence, and the shilling was twelve pence. Coins of this era were hammered and rough. Smooth, milled/machine-made coins didn't emerge until the 17th century.

Purchasing Power:

- Knight's armour (complete) – L16 6s 8d
- A book – L1
- A cow – 10s
- Rent (cottage) – 5s per year
- Linen – 1s
- Wine (good quality) – 8d per gallon
- Pair of gloves – 7d
- Candles (tallow) – 1.5d

Regency England Currency

When we speed along to the Regency era's currency, we still have pounds, shillings and pence. The values were made up of:

- 20 shillings in a pound
- 240 pence in a pound
- 12 pence in a shilling
- 5 shillings in a crown
- 4 crowns = a pound
- 21 shillings = a guinea

Purchasing Power:

- 3-volume novel – 15s (approx. £34 today, or 5 days' wages of a skilled tradesman)
- 2 volumes of scripture – 14s
- Silk stockings – 12s
- Simple white dress – 5s
- Pair of gloves – 4s

Gloves went up from pence to shillings, as an example of the difference between those two eras. Inflation, eh? Books went down from a pound to 15 shillings, though – that'll be owing to that marvellous printing press again.

By the way, the UK "went metric" in 1965. Our coins went through decimalisation to give us our modern 100 pence to the pound system. No more shillings!

Our measurements…let's just say it's complicated; there are the things we're supposed to use and things we stubbornly cling onto e.g. we still think of milk and beer in pints but water in litres. We know what meters are, but if you ask a Brit how tall they are, they will probably give you their height in feet and inches. Similarly, our body weight is still in stones, even though we use kilograms and grams in recipes. Hey, I never said we're not weird!

~ How much do items cost your characters?
~ Which currency do they use?

Education

For too long, people did not receive formal education as we understand it. Wealthy children were often sent from home for instruction, on matters such as how to run a household - girls often became ladies' maids in another house in the medieval era and learned that way. Boys could be sent to train to be a knight, receive ecclesiastical instruction, or study the law. These children would usually be around the age of 7-10 when they were sent away.

The poor learned what they needed to survive, essentially – this was often farm-related. From around the 12th century, master craftsmen could take on apprentices.

It wasn't until 1880 that the UK made schooling compulsory. However, educational institutions have long existed. The first cathedral schools here date back to Saxon times, around 598 AD. Edward VI instituted free grammar schools in Tudor England. But, sadly, child labour was a thing, and this kept most poor families sending their offspring to such schools. Eton College was established in 1491.

Remember, the Church controlled most of the writing until the 15th century. Scribes were used in households to read and write accounts and correspondence.
Fun fact - Due to high levels of illiteracy, shops used to display signs outside, depicting an emblem of their trade/guild. And a few remain even now.

~ So, how well-educated are your characters?
~ Were they able to attend some form of school?
~ Or have they learned more practical knowledge from an authority figure?
~ Can they read and write?
~ What job do they have?

Health

So, you have a socio-economic background sorted. This will guide you as to their general state of health.

Life expectancy from the medieval to Regency eras was around thirty-five years old, across much of Europe. Now, it is important to factor in the exceptionally high infant mortality rate. If you reached your twentieth birthday, you'd be likely to see your fiftieth. The Victorians fared a little better, with their average life expectancy increasing to around forty-eight by the end of that period.

The changing life expectancy plays a part in **what age they were expected to marry**. I'm sorry to say that for a long time, women were marriageable once they showed signs of being ready to conceive i.e. they began to menstruate. Marriage, after all, was there to help with procreation.

In Ancient Greece, females could be 14 or 16 years old, whilst the males were 18-24.

Ancient Roman brides, generally speaking, had to be at least 12 years old. If they were over 25, they could marry without parental consent.

Up until the French Revolution, the marriageable age was 12 for females (and 14 for males). This increased in 1792 to age 13. In 1804, it went up to 15. And then 18 in 2006, to bring it in line with males.

The UK marriageable age wasn't really legally dictated until **the Marriage Act of 1753**, which merely stated that a person under the age of 21 must have the consent of parents or guardians. It also stipulated that ceremonies must be conducted in a parish church or chapel of the Church of England and that banns must've been called or a licence obtained. Females may have been married as young as 12 and boys 14.

In 1929, Parliament (UK) stipulated the minimum age for both sexes was 16, with parental consent (and 21 without it). But I have seen it quoted that the age was raised to 16 in 1756. And now, in 2022, the age has been raised to 18.

NB Just because they could get married at those ages, didn't mean they did. The average marital age has changed over time. It's worth double-checking your chosen time period's average. Also, this is marriageable age, not the age of (sexual) consent.

But, getting back to actual health matters... we like to think of ourselves as far superior in terms of health care. And granted, we generally live longer and healthier. But before dismissing the old ways entirely, deaths after medical intervention remains pretty similar between now and the 15th century!

It's worth checking your chosen time period for plague, disease, pandemic etc. Is your character safe? Or are they likely to fall prey to some ghastly illness? And if they do, what are their chances of survival? And which medical treatments would they be likely to receive? Eek!

If you want to really worry, take a look at pain medication. Mind you, laudanum was a great idea in principle – shame about all the addiction!? Oh, pretty poppy – you are not so innocent as you appear.

If you have a female lead, is she going to get pregnant? Can she survive childbirth? Without gas & air? Double eek!

Medical thinking during the medieval era sought to temper the four humors of the body:

- ❖ Sanguine (Blood)
- ❖ Choleric (Yellow Bile)
- ❖ Melancholic (Black Bile)
- ❖ Phlegmatic (Phlegm)

These were represented by the four elements and manifested in the body as hot, cold, dry and moist. And they could be interrupted by, yes, disease, but also demons, gods, witchcraft and astronomical events.

From the 12th century, schools of surgery were gradually introduced. These were more medically trained than the barber-surgeons who performed things such as bloodletting, tooth-pulling and wound-stitching.

The medical surgeon was instructed on air, diet, exercise and drugs. The wise ones treated the wounds with vinegar or alcohol. But, they were fairly rare, as they were held liable for any fatality which resulted. And there were quite a few mishaps without antibiotics etc.

However, these surgeons performed rapid amputations for those injured in battle - the quicker the better for the patient, to stop the loss of blood. And they made a rudimentary cast for broken limbs too.

Bloodletting was performed in cases of fever, as clearly there was too much blood (heat) in the body!? It was a practice which lasted a long time, so maybe it helped (*shrugs*).

Sweating was a way of ridding the body of excess fluid - fires, piles of blankets, hot cloths...all could be applied to encourage sweat.

Inducing vomiting or issuing a laxative were also deemed fine ways of ridding the body of those nasty excess humors.

Wine was seen as a restorative, so it wasn't all bad (*wink wink*).

Along with physical treatments, prayer and penance were prescribed remedies, y'know, in case God was punishing the patient.

Wise women had known for centuries of the healing properties of plants. And even monks, who administered medical remedies as charity, grew physik/physic gardens.

They grew herbs such as:
- Dandelion
- Elecampane
- English Lavender
- Lovage
- Mallow
- Myrtle
- Pennyroyal
- Sage
- St. John's Wort
- Thyme
- Vervain
- Yarrow

Sadly, some of the plants were, in fact, toxic, so hindered rather than cured.

Willow bark, honey, cobwebs, moss and **live snails** were in the general home first aid kit.

Willow bark was a painkiller and may even have helped reduce inflammation.

Honey was readily available. Its stickiness helped bind wounds whilst stopping them from drying out. Turns out, it has antimicrobial properties too, so not as silly as it first sounds.

Now, cobwebs are astonishing. I sniffed at the thought, because eww! But, if it was clean, then the sticky web may have actually helped wounds. It would bind them together, and contain antiseptic and antifungal properties. The vitamin K in cobwebs may help blood clotting too - well, I never!

Snails would be used to treat minor cuts and burns. It's been discovered that their slime does indeed contain antiseptic, anaesthetic, antibiotic, and antiviral properties, along with collagen and elastin. So good is this icky substance, that it's now being put back into cosmetics.

Isabel in "Love in the Roses" has recourse to use blood moss. This is used to soak up her menstrual flow. This actually happened in real life! Its technical term is sphagnum moss and was used for that and to mop up blood from wounds.

From around 1803, opium as an alkaloid morphine was introduced to the medicine cabinet. But of course, opium poppies were well known before that, since 3,400 BC when the Sumerians cultivated it in Mesopotamia and called it the "joy plant". It travelled to the Ancient Egyptians and Minoans. Traders took the opium flowers to Carthage, and Europe, where it spread to Persia, India and China. In the 16th century, it was turned into laudanum. Today, opiates can be found in the form of codeine. Great for pain relief, bad for addiction.

Trepanning (or trephination) has been used since neolithic times. This is the procedure of drilling a hole into the patient's skull to relieve headaches, pressure or epilepsy. Most people actually survived! And, before you scoff, it's still in use today.

However, it's now part of neurosurgery – craniotomies – to remove epidural and subdural hematomas (brain bleeds). The removed piece of skull is normally replaced as quickly as possible, and kinder, modern surgical instruments are used.

We seem to have waited until the 19th century to fully realise cleanliness was important to avoid killing one's patients. Germs were also being discussed, essentially for the first time.

A Brief History of Medicine

- ❖ 4000 BC - Origins of Ayurveda
- ❖ 2600 BC - Imhotep – Ancient Egypt's priest-physician (later deified as a god of medicine)
- ❖ 1800 BC - Kahun Gynecological Papyrus
- ❖ 700 BC - Knidos medical school (and one at Cos), Greece
- ❖ 500-300 BC - Hippocrates (of Cos) wrote the first Hippocratic oath. It's still in use today, although somewhat different to back then. However, "do no harm" still lies at its heart.
- ❖ 129-216 BC - Galen – Greek physician, surgeon and scholar of the Roman Empire, whose findings formed a complete medical philosophy which dominated medicine throughout the Middle Ages until the beginning of the modern era
- ❖ 1030 - Avicenna - The Canon of Medicine - remained a standard textbook in Muslim and European universities until the 18th century
- ❖ 1084 - first documented hospital in England, in Canterbury
- ❖ 1100-1300 - medical schools were founded in Europe; Bologna, Montpellier, Oxford, Paris and Salerno
- ❖ 1249 - Roger Bacon writes about convex lens spectacles for treating long-sightedness
- ❖ 1260 - Louis IX established Les Quinze-Vingt; originally a retreat for the blind, it became a hospital for eye diseases and is now one of the most important medical centres in Paris

- Early 16th century - Paracelsus, an alchemist by trade, rejects occultism and pioneers the use of chemicals and minerals in medicine. Burns the books of Avicenna, Galen and Hippocrates.
- 1518 - Henry VIII, by royal charter, founded the Royal College of Physicians of London – he actually did a good thing!
- 1570–1643 - John Woodall - Ship surgeons used lemon juice to treat scurvy
- 1590 - Microscope was invented
- 1628 - William Harvey explains the circulatory system in Exercitatio Anatomica de Motu Cordis et Sanguinis in Animalibus
- 1736 - Claudius Aymand performs the first successful appendectomy
- 1766 - The New Jersey Medical Society became the first medical organisation in the USA
- 1774 - Joseph Priestley discovers nitrous oxide, nitric oxide, ammonia, hydrogen chloride and oxygen
- 1796 - Edward Jenner develops a smallpox vaccination method
- 1816 - Rene Laennec invents the stethoscope
- 1831 - Chloroform was invented (reportedly popularised by Queen Victoria in the 1850s)
- 1846 - First painless surgery with general anaesthetic
- 1847 - The American Medical Association (AMA) was established
- 1847 - Ignaz Semmelweis discovers how to prevent puerperal (childbed) fever
- 1870 - Louis Pasteur and Robert Koch establish the germ theory of disease
- 1895 - Wilhelm Conrad Röntgen discovers the use of X-rays in medical imaging

- 1927 - First vaccines for tuberculosis and tetanus
- 1930 - First successful sex reassignment surgery performed in Dresden, Germany
- 1935 – Gas and Air machine developed
- 1948 - NHS founded in the UK

Doctors

When your character is poorly, who are they going to call (avoids Ghostbusters joke opportunity)?

I'm going to use my Regency definitions here, as they're at an interesting point of medical change.

- Physicians – were considered the most desirable as they had further education and apprenticeship. Being so learned, they were considered gentlemen. They charged high fees.
- Surgeons – sort of like our modern GP and would treat lesser mortals. Would perform crude forms of surgery
- Apothecaries – think of these as dispensing chemists or pharmacists. They would grind ingredients into powders and tinctures.
- Midwives / Accoucheurs – The male midwife was introduced. Viewed as educated and trusted by the nobility
- Barbers / Dentists – I say dentist, but they pulled teeth and that was about it

But there have been a variety of options throughout history, as you can glean from the above. Wise women, barber-surgeons, and physicians are amongst the most common, historically speaking.

Calling for the doctor would require payment, though. And they were still viewed with suspicion, seen as killing as many as they saved, even into the 19th century.

Until the male personage inserted himself into the field of midwifery, women most commonly used a birthing stool. This clever chair was a horseshoe shape, so the person in labour could squat and let gravity assist. It appears the menfolk introduced the lying down method. Just saying.

Forceps
These first appeared in England and Scotland in 1735. They were actually invented in the 1600s but sadly kept under wraps. They were an important advancement in childbirth as they helped with difficult births, once the midwives learned the correct pressure to use. They then saw a steep decline in use from the mid-1900s. But, back when caesareans were incredibly perilous, these instruments must've saved many lives.

~ How old are your characters?
~ And what age are they likely to live to?
~ What is the average marital age in their time?
~ What medical care do they have access to?
~ What disease/illness are they likely to contract?

Food, Water & Hygiene

Mmm...food – one of my favourite topics.

Money has always dictated standards of healthcare. But the further back you go, the availability of food also plays an important role – feast or famine was an actual thing.

What was available when?

e.g. In the 15th century, rich people tended to eat a diet based on meat and fish (not much veg) with white bread, and the poor subsisted on tough brown bread and vegetables. The poor should have been healthier, looking at this, but they had far more dangerous, manual labour and scanter pickings of food.

Poor people would usually have a pot continuously bubbling over the fire, to which they'd add scraps and grains. Cottagers grew their own vegetables, and items such as cabbage were common. Other things such as vetches (pea family) and the occasional bits of meat were included. I bet it smelled lovely (*pinches nose*). This dish was generally called pottage, but even richer homes had variations of this.

Incidentally, there were designated flesh (meat) and fish days in the 15th century. Wednesdays, Fridays and Saturdays were supposed to be meat-free. And then there were additional fast and feast days of religious significance. Due to long periods of abstinence, such as Lent and Advent, people of the Middle Ages fasted for around 40% of the year.

However, as people ate more fish, it depleted the stocks. In the south of France, fishing was forbidden during the summer, when salt was harvested from the coastal marshes. From the second half of the thirteenth century, the kings of France issued legislation to prevent overfishing. Sustainability; not a new fad!

Henry VIII took England into a reduced fish-eating period as it was "popish flesh". Well, he changed the religion and could make his own rules, right? But, his son, Edward VI reinstated fast days to help the suffering fishermen – this seemed to dictate fish days on Fridays, Saturdays and Lent (fish for forty days straight, anyone? Yuck!). Fish Fridays are still a tradition in some Catholic households.

Talking of Lent, it gave us the Full English Breakfast (sort of). On Collop Monday (the day before Shrove Tuesday), people would use up any meat (usually pork/bacon) and cook it with eggs for dinner. Bit of a stretch, but the idea pleases me that this is where we got the Full Monty.

England had to wait until the 17th century before eating a proper breakfast, regardless of social class. And certainly, the Industrial Revolution of the 19th century nudged the working classes into eating a full breakfast to sustain themselves. Of course, we had Mr John Kellogg in the 20th century who gave us the idea of breakfast cereal.

"The best thing since sliced bread" is a common phrase. We didn't get it until the 1950s, along with electric toasters. Before that, bread was speared onto toasting forks and held in front of a fire. This is also when instant coffee started to emerge – hoorah!

What time is lunch/dinner?

The actual word "lunch" wasn't in common use until the 19th century. Between the 17th century and then, it was "nuncheon". The French of the 17th century gave us "souper" as a light meal at noon – the English copied them. In the 1750s, the Earl of Sandwich is said to have given us our sandwich; a handheld snack to be eaten, possibly whilst gaming.

Now, I got to thinking…their 'dinner' (main meal) would probably then have been at midday (for the rich, at least). Poor roads and no lighting with guests having to travel long distances? Makes sense to dine together with as much natural light as possible. There are historians who concur and some who differ.

And for the record, they had rigid table manners in place. It may be fun to watch the likes of Henry VIII gnaw on chicken legs in films. However, one would slice meat with one's own belt knife, and gently place the food into the mouth with one's fingers – no forks. Hands would be washed before the meal, and finger bowls were on the tables. Chewing was strictly with the mouth closed (*misophonia sufferer here sighs in relief*) Napkins were placed over one's left shoulder, or those of lower rank would have it over their arm.

Breakfast

People got up at the crack of dawn for Mass. Breakfast, if anything (for it was considered gluttonous), consisted of a piece of bread and some wine. Seems fair compensation for an early start to me.

The Romans really only had one main meal at lunchtime (noon) (*tummy grumbles*).

The Georgians of the 18th century ate bread, cheese and ale first thing.

I quite like the Regency era's honey or plum cake with hot chocolate or coffee. And they did have toast – yay! But they often didn't eat their first meal until 9-10 am, so had to occupy themselves beforehand.

During the Victorian era, they favoured eggs and kidneys (*scrunches nose*).

The Edwardians are the first to truly claim a sumptuous breakfast in bed.

Artificial lighting in the 17th century saw a shift to eating later in the day. And, by the late 18th century, driven largely by working patterns, most town and city dwellers were eating three meals per day. During the 19th century, the main meal started to be eaten in the evening. But a good old Sunday roast can still be enjoyed to this day at noon, even if church-going has dwindled.

If one attended a ball in the Regency era, their lavish dinner was served between 6-8 pm. With a light supper at the end, around 10 pm. Because of these late times, young ladies would eat a nuncheon at noon, to sustain them throughout all that dancing.

What's on the menu?
Along with the clothes, food was also brightly coloured in the Middle Ages – red, yellow and blue could have been seen at table.

It was, of course, seasonal. Beef and pork were available all year. And the high-status folks also had veal and capon (castrated cockerel). Swans, herons and peacocks could be eaten on grand occasions too.

Pigeon was only eaten in the summer. Suckling pig was available from December to July. Chicken, pheasant and duck were most common.

A vast array of fish was on the menu (the sea and freshwater kinds). Herrings were popular, and when they were scarce, one could order barrels of sturgeon. Oysters were plentiful and cheap, at least until the cost went up at Christmas due to the high demand.

There were even different cheeses. The first recorded Cheddar was in 1500. A farmer's/cottage cheese was probably the most common.

Herbs and spices were grown in kitchen gardens or ordered in. Things such as saffron and mace were surprisingly well-used. As were honey and salt.

Rich households had sauciers who made a tasty selection of sauces to go with one's bountiful meat. Pastry chefs may also have been employed. (I'm starting to salivate!).

But, oh, and (*gasp*), they had… no potatoes, tomatoes or…or…(*sobs*) coffee or tea!! How did they live? Have mercy! Potatoes and tomatoes were brought in during the 16th century. Europeans didn't get to have coffee or chocolate until the 17th century – a social injustice if ever I saw one (*winky face*). Cakes, as we know them started emerging in the 18th century – before that, they were more bread-like really. The glorious croissant arrived in France in 1829.

To be fair, our diet didn't change massively until we began importing more.

Drink/Water

Water was not for drinking?

Well, in 4,000 BC, there are records showing that people knew to boil water before it was safe to drink.

A Spartan in the 9th century made a cup which made mud stick to the side. Hippocrates invented a "Hippocrates Sleeve" – a cloth bag to strain boiled rainwater. And the Romans gave the world aqueducts which carried fresh water. However, these were ill-used once the Romans left England, and disease ran rampant. So, we were back to drinking wine or ale/beer.

In the 17th and 18th centuries, purification via water filtration became a thing. Scotland, in 1804, had the first municipal water purifying plant in the world which used gravel filters. It distributed its clean water via horse and cart.

It wasn't until the 19th century that people on a global scale truly appreciated the importance of clean water again, and water treatment plants began to be built. In 1974, the US passed the Safe Drinking Water Act, ensuring all citizens had access to clean drinking water.

Slightly unsavoury to mention it after food and drink, but... umm... **sanitation**. What goes in must come out!? There was a chap named John Snow and he knew something; he realised (in 1854) that cholera was spread by contaminated water. The removal of a contaminated water pump in Soho, London, led to the cessation of an epidemic.

Edwin Chadwick in 1849 brought in reform. He introduced piped drinking water into homes – yay. And also introduced flushed sewage systems – yay. However, said sewage was pumped into the river Thames and contaminated the water supply – boo and oops.

Which leads me to toilets. The first modern, flushing toilet was introduced to England in 1596 in Queen Elizabeth I's castle, by John Harrington. It wasn't popular though and didn't catch on until the mid-19th century.

Around 3100BC, in Ancient Egypt, the wealthy had indoor toilets made of limestone which had a pit underneath it. In 2000 BC, the clever Minoans in Crete flushed toilets with water.

The Romans developed sewers in 800BC – rows of benches were put in toilet rooms where people could sit side-by-side to evacuate their bowels. However, there was no toilet paper, so they used a sponge on a stick.

In the 12th century, monks living in Portchester Castle, England had stone chutes taking their waste to the sea. Well, it's right there. Generally, castles had a garderobe or privy - a glorified hole, with probably a plank of wood atop it (with a hole in). Some jutted out of the house wall, on a platform. But they all had to lead somewhere; chutes took the...err..waste down to a cesspit or moat. Straw or rags were used for...wiping. A window was happily situated to help alleviate the odour. Bars were in situ to stop intruders from entering via the chutes. Peasants would have a midden heap where they would empty their chamber pots and any other waste e.g. animal bones and mollusc shells. In cities, they just emptied their waste out the window, into the street (eww!).

In 1848, the UK decided every new home should have a water closet (WC) or ash-pit privy. These were outdoors in most cases (brr!).

Just because everyone loves his name; Thomas Crapper installed lavatories in royal palaces in 1861.

It wasn't until the 20th century that toilets were finally brought inside for the mainstream populace.

Toilet paper, incidentally, has a varied history. The ingenious folk in China invented a form of toilet paper in the 2nd century BC, which was widely used by the 6th century. However, the modern form of it was made in 1391.

Mass manufacture of toilet paper didn't start until the 19th century. Joseph C. Gayetty in New Jersey, US, created the first commercially packaged toilet paper in 1857 – just loose paper sheets. And in 1879, British businessman, Walter Alcock created perforated paper on a roll.

Seeing as I've wandered into the realm of hygiene here, I may as well mention **cleanliness**. Allegedly, it's next to godliness, after all. The grubby image we have in mind of everyone pre-bathrooms may not be entirely accurate. Cleanliness has actually been highly rated for a long time, just maybe not quite to our standards.

We could take a trip to Ancient Rome. I've been to Pompeii and have seen the public bathing houses. The, um, slightly lurid images of genitalia by the (what's thought to be) clothes pegs, seem to strongly hint at more than just washing took place there. Ahem, there were also spaces for games, libraries, galleries, meditation rooms and lecture halls at these venues. Some of which could house up to 6,000 bathers at once.

In cities such as Bath, UK, natural hot springs supplied the hot water to the Roman baths. It was a ritualistic process, involving a sort of skin scraping with a blunt knife, massaging with oil and rinsing with hot water.

At around the same time, there were bath houses for Buddhist monks in temples in India, presumably for ceremonial cleansing.

The very hot Turkish Bath (similar to the Roman process) is associated with the Ottoman Empire.

The rich amongst the medieval folk of England had a stone chamber usually called The Lord's Bath. This housed large wooden barrels which servants would fill with heated water and herbs. A pipe may have carried waste water away. Complete with a dressing area and ledges for accessories, presumably not a rubber ducky though.

There were even public bath houses in many towns. Again, many tales of prostitution hover around these too. From images I've seen, maybe even monks weren't immune to their charms! Well, lots of naked bodies all together; it's a great temptation. This is probably why the religious orders started murmuring about immersion in water being a sin as it allowed the devil to enter your body. Dude, if you can't keep your eyes and urges to yourself, it's not anyone's fault but your own!

Anyway, peasants in the countryside probably dunked in streams. But most people would have had access to some sort of bowl and cloth to have a wipe down of essential body parts.

Soap, incidentally, was known and made in England as far back as the 10th century.

The first bathtub seems to have emerged in the Palace of Knossos, Crete c. 1900 BC – ingenious folk! However, it wasn't until 1883 that the Standard Sanitary Manufacturing Company (now American Standard) and John Michael Kohler, in the USA, began to enamel cast iron tubs with the clawfoot design we're more familiar with.

~ What do your characters eat and when?
~ And what did they have to drink?
~ Where did they go to the loo?
~ How did they bathe?

Religion & Celebration

I appreciate the topic of religion can be a sensitive one. However, your character may be very pious/devout.

One does need to consider the main religion of the country your book is set in. At differing times, this will have led to upheaval and perhaps persecution (*squints at Henry VIII again*).

And, as previously mentioned, religion may well have an effect on dress codes and/or laws.

However, the reason for my mentioning it in the 'who' section is more to do with celebrations; the nicer side. Following on from this example, those in Medieval Europe had many saints' days to honour. And what better way to do that than with a big party to impress your neighbours, and to hopefully help your cause in the afterlife?

The mainstays of Christmas and Easter may be of note to your characters. Except 1647-1660 when Christmas was banned in England and maybe some other Puritan zones; or maybe even then (because people did rebel), do your people celebrate that wonderful time of worship and feasting?

Food is often tied in with big events. Before turkeys were first brought to England in 1523, rich people had boar, venison or beef at Christmas, for example. Mince pies go way back but originally contained actual minced meat.

Gateau-type cakes came into being around the mid-nineteenth century. Before refined sugar and baking powder, cakes were more like sweetened bread but did exist. And fruit pies have long been an option.

Be aware of the long fast periods e.g. Lent. No meat, only fish was to be consumed for the forty days before Easter.

What about christenings, funerals and weddings? Are there any, and how are they marked?

Or maybe they're not Christian and have other religious festivals/observances? Hannukah, Passover, Diwali and Eid-al-Fitr are amongst the options.

Of course, not all celebrations are related to religion. Are there any birthdays for your character to enjoy? And if yes, how do they do so?

~ What do your characters celebrate?
~ Is there cake, and if so, what kind?
~ Are there any other dishes made for the special occasion?

WHO - TASK

The people! Finally, we get to see your characters.

~ What is your main character's name?
~ What do they look like (features)?
~ What do they sound like?
~ What are they wearing?
~ How old are they?
~ What background do they come from (and do they stay in that sphere)?
~ Do they have a title?
~ Where do they live?
~ How well educated are they?
~ Are they healthy?
~ What disease/illness are they likely to contract?
~ What medical care do they have access to?
~ What do they eat/drink?
~ Do they celebrate anything nice?

WRITING

The Story Basics

OK, now you have the framework and key things in your mind, it's time to write your story. But you will need a:

Plot

In its simplest form, you need a:
- Beginning
- Middle
- End

Simple, right? Let us delve a little deeper.

There are whole books which explore these 'story beats' in-depth. But I'm providing some high-level hints to get you started, at least.

Beginning

Before all else, you need an enticing first line and paragraph. This is your "hook". Readers will very quickly judge whether your book is worth reading. They have the option to "look inside" before even buying on Amazon. Even then, they may not get past the first page.

So, make sure you offer an element of mystery. Why does the person need to read this book?

And make it clean! Not as in not smutty. Be extra sure that there are no spelling or grammatical errors on that first page.

And start the story right. What motivates your main character?

It's time to start bringing your person to life.

It's not much of a story without a challenge or two. So, as mean as it may make you feel, give your character something to overcome. How they start should be different from how they finish, hopefully for the better at the end.

They need at least one of these:
- ❖ a character flaw to be fixed
- ❖ a goal - what they want to achieve
- ❖ a lesson – what do they learn?

There should be a presenting problem and an underlying cause.

What stands in the way of them achieving their goal? And how do they get around it? This should create your inciting incident; the moment your book pivots around.

By around 10% of the way through your book (within the first couple of chapters), you should have an inciting incident; a catalyst which spurs your main character into action – sets the theme.

~ How does your character feel on page one?
~ What is their major obstacle going to be?

Middle

Around a quarter of the way through, your character should be on their path, starting to experience the challenges you've set for them. And they should have someone who will aid them in their quest.

At the halfway point, maybe they could have a false victory. The stakes get raised, and they grow more determined to succeed.

~ What steps have they now taken?
~ And what will they do next?

End

And in the final quarter, maybe your character hits rock bottom. They're knocked down and need to reflect on all that has happened and come up with a new solution. Ding! They've learned their main lesson.

So that in the very last moments they can show the difference from their start to now. What wonderful accomplishment/s have they achieved?

~ Hoorah! They've achieved their aim – time to celebrate
~ Think back to page one – how is that different to the last page?

Also, there is a tricky balance to be struck with historical folk. They absolutely need to live in their own age; this means sometimes doing things which we don't necessarily agree with today. However, our readers are modern, and we should take care not to insult or injure them. So, make your characters realistic, but maybe give them some politically correct parameters.

Not everyone thinks the same way today. Spoiler alert – they never did! Political and religious views etc. have always differed. There have always been debates, disputes and/or wars.

Some people will tell you, "They wouldn't have said/done that back then," but how do they know? They weren't there. This is in the context of behaviour. Be careful not to include modern slang/terminology/technology.

e.g. A favourite one is people declaring sex out of wedlock a big no-no. However, there is historical evidence to show that people have always had sex outside of marriage. It just wasn't the norm at times. Whilst at others, particularly amongst the poor, it was secretly encouraged so the family knew the girl could get pregnant!

My particular favourite is looking into the minds of women throughout the ages. The image they presented to outsiders was often very different from how they appeared behind closed doors. At some point, we were taught that women were meek – I challenge that.

Having all this knowledge, take care not to become a history teacher. All these background things you're now thinking about may never even be mentioned directly. But you, as the author, need to know because it gives your characters a framework in which to live. Do NOT go overly into detail about every little thing. Unless it's pertinent to the story, your reader doesn't need to know the manufacturer of the furniture or crockery. In short…

DO NOT INFO DUMP!

Think about the conversations you have in daily life. Do you reference a specific price or maker? If you wouldn't, your character probably wouldn't either.

Tropes

What is a trope? I don't much like the word, but it is a useful concept. In Book Land, it has come to mean, *"describing commonly recurring literary and rhetorical devices, motifs or clichés in creative works."* Simply put, a theme of sorts.

Historical Romance Tropes:

- Friends or Enemies to Lovers - This pair is either in the friend or enemy zone, but something changes, forcing a change of perspective and suddenly passion ignites. How did they not see it before?
- Fake Relationships - To keep family off their backs, the couple hatches a plan to pretend to be engaged, but oops, they actually fall in love.
- Marriage of Convenience - Whether the marriage was formed as a business deal or to hide one partner's sexuality, love was not originally there, but maybe it could emerge in some way.
- Damaged & Healing Hero - Aww, the poor person has been downtrodden and injured. Only your MC can save them!
- Compromising Position - Oh my, how scandalous. Your MC has broken the rules of Society. What will people say?
- Destined to be Together / Lovers Reunited - There really is no choice – this pair just have to be together, no matter who/what gets in their way.

- ❖ Forbidden Love - Who is Society to declare this pair should not be together? Their love is true, despite what others think. So what if she's a governess and he's an earl? They will risk family and fortune to be united.

- ❖ Secretly Rich - The hero shuns the false modesty of those thrown at them. In order to be seen and loved for who they truly are, they will conceal their riches and/or identity.

- ❖ Rogues and Rakes - Who doesn't love a bad boy? But can he be tamed? Was he really just misunderstood?

These are tropes for a reason. They are not things to avoid like the plague. They are to be embraced and even toyed with – have fun with whichever one tickles your fancy. But remember the HEA (happy ever after) aim.

Historical **Fiction** Tropes:

- ❖ Historical Person – there is a real-life famous person you're putting into your fictional world, what fun! Just be careful not to bring their good name into ill repute!

- ❖ Major Event/Political Rebellion – maybe a historical event is your focal point e.g. a war or civil movement; things are going to change around here. There's a whirlwind that people are going to get sucked into. Who will survive the turmoil?

- ❖ Religious Figurehead – for better or worse, there is a character whose faith is strong and they are going to make their voice heard. Preach!

- ❖ The Unseen Servant – you're in the future, and maybe know things about a certain servant others didn't realise about them in their own time. Now their story can be safely told by you. Oh, the things they've seen!

- ❖ Ahead of Their Time – your character is too advanced for their era and seeks to be the change they want to see in the world. Go get 'em!

- ❖ Marriage – whether your character is avoiding matrimony or entering into a marriage of convenience, this story pivots around the subject of getting hitched. Ooh, what's their reason?

- ❖ Timehop – maybe there are two timelines covered in your story, highlighting differences but with one thing linking the two, such as an object/heirloom. How do your characters interact with this item?

Characters

The battle between good and evil is a story as old as time. So, who are your goodies and who are your baddies?

Your main character, the protagonist, does not act alone. So, who are their cohorts? Is there someone who is by their side through thick and thin? Or comes in at the last moment to help them save the day?

And who stands in their way? The opposing side, the antagonist.

Is your main character even the good person? Or are they a loveable rogue of some kind?

NB Main characters kinda need to be likeable, but they don't have to start out as a goody two shoes.

~ Are there any parents/guardians around?
~ Or maybe even an animal sidekick? Hey, it could happen – Greyfriars Bobby springs to mind.

Characteristics

Remember, if you name a character, you should describe them, and fairly soon after introducing them so that your reader doesn't picture them one way, only to be frustrated by your contrary definition later. But don't info dump it all at once. You can introduce bits of description in thoughts or dialogue of people around them throughout your story. Or, sparingly, in mirrors (this gets old fast though, and is currently out of favour).

A lot of readers don't like excessive description. But some basics are always good, and then you can let your readers' imagination fill in the rest. Choose maybe two or three things:

- Hair
- Eyes
- Height
- Age (at least general impression of)
- Build

But make it distinctive. How can you describe a feature once which will stick in your readers' minds so you don't have to repeat it? Seriously, don't be repetitive with descriptions.

As previously mentioned, I find it useful to have a saved picture of what I think my characters should look like. I note down everything about them, but don't necessarily use it all. I need to know, but readers only require the most important aspects.

There are other things which make people unique and are arguably more important than basic appearance:

- Facial expressions
- Hand gestures
- Deportment

Is there something your characters do which makes them stand out? Do they scratch their nose when nervous? Perhaps they remain silent unless they feel they have something important to divulge or witter away without needing any response whatsoever? Maybe they point their fingers a certain way? Walk with firm strides, a swagger or a limp? I'll go into more detail about body language in the 'Writing Tips' section.

Possessions

Does your character wear especially fine clothes? Side note - I'm always wary of people without a single crease in their outfit - LOL. Or perhaps their garments are badly mended/patched? Do their outfits cause admiration or scorn?

Vehicles can tell you a lot about a person. Even in a time before cars, carriages and even horses had snob value.

What is their house like? Big or small? Finely decorated, or as sparse as Scrooge's pad? Maybe they have more than one place of residence? Or perhaps there is mould on the wall and a drip coming through the ceiling?

Even the food people eat could give hints. Extravagant feasts? A pineapple in Regency England was a very showy offy item - sometimes only on display and not eaten.

Basically, show don't tell is the best way forward with descriptions.

STORY - TASK

~ How is your main character (MC) flawed?
~ And how are they going to overcome those flaws?
~ Who will help?
~ For romance novels; how do they meet their love interest and what do they look like and behave?
~ Choose a trope
~ What does the new, improved version of your MC look like in the end?
~ And who are the side characters (role, behaviour and appearance)?
~ How do they present themselves to the world?

Writing Tips

Save!

OK, number one rule; save your work regularly!

Have auto-save activated and check that it's working. Occasionally, hit that 'save' button anyway.

And back your work up. Save it to your desktop and the cloud and maybe an external hard drive too. Have more than one save location, is what I'm saying. Because if your PC/laptop dies, you will cry uncontrollably if you lose your work. Trust me! No, really, I know (*sobs*).

YOU CANNOT SAVE TOO OFTEN!

Tense

Keep your past behind you!

- Past: Tricia bought a book
- Present: Tricia is buying a book
- Future: Tricia will buy a book

What I sometimes see is:

- Tricia went to the shop and is buying a book. She paid at the till and left with her treasure in her grasp.

But Tricia isn't "buying", as the sentence is in the past tense. It should read:

- Tricia went to the shop and bought a book.

You can write dialogue in the present tense and keep the narrative in the past tense. But keep that narrative in the past.

Of course, you may choose to write your book in the present tense. Absolutely your choice. Just stick to whichever one you choose. At least in the same sentence and/or paragraph.

There is the possibility of mixing tenses, but these need to be carefully done and split with a scene change.

First Person vs Third Person

Whilst we're talking tense, let's also think about point of view (POV). Is your character narrating their own novel (first person)? Or are you, the author, an omniscient presence (3rd person)?

Be wary of head-hopping in either case - giving one person's perspective and then rapidly changing to another is very disorienting.

Increasingly, authors are choosing more than one first-person narrative. This is usually, and best done, in separate, clearly labelled chapters for each character. It's actually quite fun.

Readers have their own preference. And that's OK. You are never going to please everyone. Just write which POV you feel your book needs.

Senses

To fully immerse readers in your world, use all the senses.
- ❖ What can your characters see?
- ❖ What do their fingers touch?
- ❖ What was that noise?
- ❖ What can they smell?
- ❖ And what do they taste?

Let your reader feel like they're there with your characters, experiencing what they do.

Maybe there is a tannery nearby - oof, yuck! Or someone wears a particular perfume? Is there a warm fire on a cold day? Does that musty smoke fill someone's nostrils? Do horse hooves clatter through the streets? Do peddlers shout their wares? How richly berried is the wine?

Dialogue

This is something I often see authors getting into a mess with.

And even I (yes, I'm human and make mistakes) had inadvertently made errors with something which should be very simple. And this is why editors are marvellous!

Basically, use a comma if you are introducing a "s/he said" type statement (a dialogue tag).

- ❖ The dialogue tag can be at the start or the end:

Lowering his voice to a whisper, he told her, "I have to tell you something."

Or "I have to tell you something," he whispered.

There is nothing wrong with using "said". It's simple and unobtrusive. Just don't overuse it. Everything in moderation. Please do not overuse dialogue tags, full stop. Just once in a while to illustrate who is talking, or to emphasise a point.

"I hate you," he yelled.

~ This does not require an exclamation mark. You are saying the character is yelling.

Generally, you should avoid exclamation marks in novels. Your writing should speak for itself.

- ❖ You can link two sentences together with a tag, by the way. You use commas for this:

"I feel so stupid," she said with a sigh, "I fell for his charm."

- ❖ You can even give them new paragraphs. Do use this sparingly, as dialogue should generally be short and snappy to increase readability. But when the same character is speaking, do not close the quotation marks at the end of the first paragraph. Just open them at the start of the new one:

"Character 1 is saying something but is going on a bit. This paragraph comes to a close, but they need to say more. Do not close the speech marks.

"A new paragraph has started here and closes as normal."

This looks odd, but I'm assured this is the correct way of laying it out.

❖ Remember, dialogue is conversation. People do not stick to rigid formality when they speak:

"Hello. It is very nice to meet you. How are you today?"

Do you hear this when you speak to your friends, or when you're people-watching? I suspect not. Is it more like, "Hey, what's up?" or, "Alright?"

You can show points in narrative or speech, by the way. But please don't do both. It can be tiresome to have a point explained by the narrator and then again by the character.

Active Voice

Modern readers tend to favour the 'active voice.'
The technical definition of **passive voice** is, "*A form or set of forms of a verb in which the subject undergoes the action of the verb (e.g. they were killed as opposed to the active form he killed them).*"

You want your characters to do something, and not just have stuff done to them.
Passive voice has its place in writing e.g. if you don't want to reveal which character is performing the action. But as a rule of thumb, you want to be dynamic, and use 'active voice'.
Think of avoiding any form of 'to be' or 'have'. Be careful; this isn't always the case. Just keep it in mind.
Here's a humorous example of passive voice: *Why was the road crossed by the chicken?*

Here's what I find handy:

He/she/it/feeling - often lead to passive voice.
I usually write in the 3rd person. So, for me, a repeating occurrence of 'she' is a good indicator of passive voice. Obviously, when writing in the first person, this changes to 'I'. Aim to keep the usage down, maybe one per paragraph?

- ❖ She ran through the forest, not knowing where she was going, but she needed to get away from whatever was chasing her.

  Becomes:
- ❖ Her feet pounded against the ground as she sprinted away from her predator, without any real thought of direction.

~ Does the second example sound more dramatic? A sense of urgency has been added. The character is moving, we can almost hear pounding feet and feel her panic. You could even add some panting or rapid heartbeats.

MAKE IT DYNAMIC!

Body Language

There is a whole host of signals we give off, and they can add a wow factor to your writing. It can also help you steer clear of that dreaded passive voice mentioned above.

Posture, hand gestures, micro-expressions – they're all available.

There is a phrase which gets used a lot: "**Show don't tell.**"

Describe situations or feelings.

- ❖ Don't tell your reader your character is unfit. Show them breathing heavily, gasping for air as they walk up the stairs.
- ❖ Don't simply state your character is embarrassed. Maybe their cheeks glow a rosy red and they feel the need to hide their face.
- ❖ Your character shouldn't, "feel sad." Maybe… "Slumping onto the sofa, she gazed at the rug, tears trickling down her cheeks."

Is your character angry? Do they launch themselves up from a chair or throw their fist into someone's nose?

Does your MC have a nervous habit? Maybe they bite their lower lip, twirl or run their fingers through their hair.

What do others see when your MC is bored, confident, defensive or happy? Show us, the readers.

How do they walk? Do they radiate elegance with a glide? Roll their shoulders in a confident swagger? Maybe they creep along as if they wish to go unnoticed? Or do they use a wheelchair – 1655 was when the first self-propelled wheelchair was invented in Germany. Before that, the "invalid's chair" which was pushed by others, was invented in 1595.

Adverbs

One should avoid using too many adverbs (the words ending 'ly'). Some authors advise against them entirely.

If you say, "*He said softly,*" it is stopping some description.

Instead, maybe try, "*He whispered in her ear.*" Or even, "*His breathy tones made her quiver*".

I'm actually a fan of adverbs. They were invented; they have a special name and everything, so I think they're fine. Just, use them with caution. Is there a more elegant/dynamic way of saying what you're writing?

Spelling And Editing

Once you've written your book, utilise spellcheck/Editor within Word (other word processors are available). You can also download software such as Grammarly which will help. Word of caution; you need to have your wits about you and not blindly trust their suggestions.

You absolutely should, at least, get a proofreader. I know it can be an expense. But even if it's a friend who you know is a wordsmith, their assistance is invaluable. Your brain knows what you meant to say, so can easily miss those "smellings" (spelling errors).

You can also hire an editor. Again, not cheap, but the good ones are worth their weight in gold. But you need to know which **type of editing** you require:

- ❖ Editorial Assessment – conducted in the early stages, to give high-level guidance on strengths and weaknesses in your characters and plot.
- ❖ Developmental Editing – again, early stages, spots major plot holes or character inconsistencies
- ❖ Copy Editing – looks in finer detail at things such as word repetition and readability e.g. spelling, grammar, tense, word usage
- ❖ Line Editing – similar to copy editing, but looks more at the flow/style
- ❖ Proof Reading – spelling and layout

Increasingly, people are also utilising '**sensitivity readers**'. If your book tackles issues which may be perceived as offensive, a sensitivity reader checks for harmful stereotypes, misrepresentation of marginalised groups, insensitive language and/or bias. This is generally done at a beta reading stage (very early on).

Formatting

Oh, there's so much information on this. I'd just like to give you a few basics, though. I use Microsoft Word, so that's what the following is based on. There are plenty of other options out there, some of which will have their own in-built formatting.

I've seen some people neglect this one, and it's just not tidy…

When starting a **new chapter**, go to the end of the last one and hit 'return'/'enter'. And then, on the 'Insert' option in the ribbon, select 'Page Break'. This will make sure that your new chapter starts on its own new page.

And **chapter headings** can get their own 'Style' of 'Heading 1' (or whatever) in the ribbon from the 'Home' section. You can modify this to however you want it to look. But by selecting it as a style, it'll come up when you do the Table of Contents (ToC) later. And all your title formats can be easily changed if you decide to do so later on.

Incidentally, if you have things in the '**front matter**', such as an Introduction that you want to ensure people read, apply the 'Heading 1' style to that also. Then, the Kindle/e-reader will open on that page – otherwise, it opens on chapter 1, skipping all your good stuff.

But first in your front matter, is your title page; book and author name.

Then, ensure you include a **copyright notice** e.g.

Published in the United Kingdom by:

Steamy Kettle Publishing

First published in electronic format and in print in 2023.
Text copyright © 2023 TL Clark

All rights reserved. No portion of this book may be reproduced, stored in a retrieval system or transmitted at any time or by any means mechanical, electronic, photocopying, recording, or otherwise without prior written permission of the publisher.

The right of TL Clark to be identified as the author of this work has been asserted by her in accordance with the Copyright, Designs and Patents Act 1988.

This is a work of fiction. Names, characters, businesses, places, events, locales, and incidents are either the products of the author's imagination or used in a fictitious manner. Any resemblance to actual persons, living or dead, or actual events is purely coincidental.

Different countries have different copyright standards, so please do check those which apply to you.

Authors have now started to include an anti-AI training statement too:

NO AI TRAINING: Without in any way limiting the author's and publisher's exclusive rights under copyright, any use of this publication to "train" generative artificial intelligence (AI) technologies to generate text is expressly prohibited. The author reserves all rights to license uses of this work for generative AI training and development of machine learning language models.

This book was written by a human. No Artificial Intelligence (AI) has been used in the production of this book.

Underneath the copyright, state your paperback book's ISBN.

After that, include any acknowledgements you wish to make e.g. cover designer, editor, special supporters etc.

Next is any dedication you would like to include.

These days, you don't always need a **table of contents** (ToC). Ebooks like to have one so readers have a clickable navigation tool. But in paperbacks, you really only need a ToC if you have named your chapters.

But, to do this, click on where you want your ToC to go. Then click on the 'References' tab on the ribbon. The easiest option is to select "Automatic Table 1 (or 2)" – the difference between these two options is merely the words "table of".

If you used that 'Heading 1' on your chapter headings, your ToC will now magically appear.

Sadly, this only applies to ebooks. Paperbacks, as far as I know, still require a manual process as the automatic link upsets them.

If you are writing an introduction, this gets included last, just before your first chapter.

From front matter, we go to **back matter**.

At the end of your story, include a little '**thank you for reading**' note, with a polite plea for your reader to leave a review, and maybe include a link to the book's Amazon page in the ebook.

To get that link, you will need to upload your book and submit it to at least the pre-order stage. It will then get its ASIN (Amazon Standard Identification Number) and Amazon page. Copy the address from the web toolbar, but only to the point of "/ref" e.g. "**https://www.amazon.com/Love-Roses-Historical-Medieval-Romance-ebook/dp/B09ZV9MT22**"

Do **not** include the part after this, which looks like: "/ref=sr_1_4?crid=38OGJH7TY7HLQ&keywords=love+in+the+roses&qid=1654077945&sprefix=love+in+the+rose%2Caps%2C406&sr=8-4" as it contains a lot of stuff you don't want/need.

This shortened version is often referred to as a "**clean link**".

Highlight the wording in your book's back matter in your own electronic file, something like "leave a review here", select 'insert', 'link' – paste that 'clean' link. Save.

You will then need to re-upload and re-submit your book's manuscript from the KDP entry you already created. Don't be scared. It's OK.

Include an "**About the Author**" section, include links to your social media and your newsletter sign-up form. In your paperback, you can include a scannable QR code in place of links.

If you have **other books**, include brief details about those too. If you use Draft 2 Digital to upload your ebook, they have the option to do this automatically.

OK, let's get on to more detail about actual formatting.

<u>**Page Layout**</u>

For **e-books**, also on the 'Home' option on the ribbon, you will find **'Paragraph'**. Click on the down arrow on the bottom right there, and a pop-up window should be displayed.

My own settings are (but feel free to try different ones or seek what others recommend)...

- ❖ Alignment – Left
- ❖ Outline level – Body Text
- ❖ Indentation – Special 'first line', By '0.25cm'
- ❖ Spacing – Before '0', After '6 pt' 'Single'

This was recommended in a free 'How to Format for Kindle' book I downloaded back when I first started self-publishing. Sadly, that book is no longer available. There may well be updated recommendations, but I've just stuck with these as they work for me.

If you start a new scene mid-chapter, be sure to create a clear **scene break**.

This can be done with a double space, but that sometimes gets mashed by the conversion going into the online manuscript. And also, visually impaired readers or those with dyslexia like to have something more obvious.

A standard scene break can be a simple ***. However, I like to nab a (royalty-free) graphic and use that, matching the theme of the book; maybe a fancy filigree scroll – nothing too big; keep it clean and simple e.g.

You may also like to use something like that underneath your chapter headings if you use titles.

For **paperbacks**, formatting gets a little more complicated. Your chosen printer may have a template and/or specific advice; please do refer to that. But some things to bear in mind:

The title page will start on the right-hand side. This is technically your page 1 for printing.

You will want to start numbering your pages from the start of Chapter 1, though.

Just above your first chapter (after your ToC or Introduction), ensure you insert a 'Section Break' under 'Layout' and 'Breaks' (select 'odd page' from the dropdown).

Then you can add your page number from the footer options under 'Insert'.

Each chapter should then start on an odd-numbered page (so it's on the right-hand page).

The first paragraph of your chapter should *not* be indented, but the rest should be.

Whether you indent after a scene break or not is up for debate.

Page margins – very generally, a half-inch (1.27cm) gap all the way around. But it will vary depending on book size and printing company.

Do check the recommended page dimensions and margin spacing for your book printer e.g. Ingram Spark or Amazon.

Do check the 'Online Previewer' once you've uploaded your manuscript to KDP. It will look different once the file's converted. Check page breaks etc. appear in the correct positions. There are options to view 'Tablet', 'Phone', and 'Kindle E-reader' – I tend to go by the Kindle view as I believe that's how the majority of readers will see the e-version.

Fonts

I tend to type in Times New Roman, size 12 for my **ebooks**; personal preference.

For my **paperbacks**, I'm rather fond of Book Antiqua, size 11. But it will depend on how many words you've written and how thick you want the book to be. Garamond, Baskerville or Palatino Linotype are often recommended fonts. Again, keep it simple – don't be fancy and render your hard work illegible.

There are other things which may come up, such as which font to use if your character writes a letter. I just pop that into italics, to be honest. Italics can also be used for a character's inner monologue. We're writing historical fiction, so characters text messaging shouldn't be an issue, but yes, at least make those bold if you ever come across it, set out similar to dialogue.

Hint: the thinner the book, the cheaper the cost. But don't aim too thin, otherwise, the font will be too small to read, and the book won't feel nice to hold.

Whichever font you choose will need to be **embedded** in the pdf when you come to upload. How to check:

If you've used Word, 'save as' pdf. Open the pdf in Adobe Acrobat Reader. Go to 'menu', 'properties' and 'fonts' – this should bring up a list of all fonts used. Next to each one, you'll hopefully see the word "embedded".

You may need to purchase a **font license** to use them – Microsoft Word standard fonts appear to be OK, but always check before publishing. I'm not a legal eagle, this is not my expertise. Please do check.

You *will*, however, need to have a font license for the ones used on your *book cover* – one of the many good reasons to hire a professional designer as they should know and take care of this.

Talking of which, I go 5 x 8" (203mm x 127mm) on my paperback **trim size** for novels. I seem to recall that was what my Jane Austen books were, and I wished to emulate her; so technical!? There are a few recommendations online which include other sizes.

When formatting a 5 x 8" paperback in Word, you therefore need to change the 'paper size' to 12.7 x 20.32 cm under 'page setup'.

I use cream **paper** for those. Ingram Spark recently introduced a 'groundwood' option, which is more akin to that used by traditional publishers and is lighter and cheaper. White is generally for textbooks.

The gloss vs matt cover debate is somewhat dependent on the cover style and what the image suits.

PUBLISHING

Publishing Options

Now, there are two options to consider first...

Do you want to try getting a **traditional publisher** or become **self-published**?

There are pros and cons to both options, and it is a deeply personal choice. There is no right or wrong here. Both have their merits and their pitfalls. At the end of the day, it comes down to personal preference.

But how do you decide?

Indie Authors (Pros & Cons)

This is probably the hardest path, judging solely on the fact it's the one I chose, and I always seem to choose the path of most resistance (*rolls eyes, facepalm*).

- ❖ You are in charge of your own destiny, but this is very much restricted.
- ❖ You dictate the content of your book.
- ❖ You say when, where and how much.
- ❖ It can be overwhelming.
- ❖ ALL the balls are in your court; writing, editing, marketing etc.
- ❖ You incur all associated costs with the above.
- ❖ Maintaining a social media presence is time-consuming and draining.

- ❖ You will also find many doors are closed to you. The major newspapers/magazines/blogs don't review indie authors. And the big literary competitions only accept traditionally published books.
- ❖ Brick & mortar book shops are virtually impossible to get into. If you use print-on-demand for your paperback, the costs are high, and the stores like a 55% wholesale discount, which pretty much prices you out.

Traditional Publishers (Pros & Cons)

OK, maybe traditional publishing is the solution. All of the above sounds like very hard work.

- ❖ Success is still not guaranteed, but you may have a better chance.
- ❖ You will probably need to approach agents first – rejections are to be expected.
- ❖ They have their own editing teams etc. They can take care of a lot of this for you. (*sigh of relief*)
- ❖ However, it's still up to you to make the changes. And you may not agree with what they have to say.
- ❖ And you still have to do a lot of your own marketing. They don't have the resources to do all this for every author on their books. They may be able to assist, and maybe you'll get the opportunity to be reviewed by the big hitters. But not necessarily.

The choice is yours, at least, which to go for. Obviously, the choice of acceptance by traditional publishers is in their hands.

Just know this; WRITING IS HARD.

Whichever door you go through, and path you walk down, it is not easy. But it might just be worth it. Success is never guaranteed, but a lot of hard work is.

Important note: if you choose traditionally published, never ever pay upfront. These are what are called vanity publishers and will not do anything for you. A decent publisher will pay you!

Also, remember what I said under 'Why' about the great authors getting many rejections. Just be prepared for that.

You may hear the term, "The Big 5" in relation to traditional publishers. These are the biggest ones in the US and require you to have an agent before you approach them.

The Big 5:

- Hachette Book Group
- HarperCollins
- Macmillan Publishers
- Penguin Random House
- Simon and Schuster

To get a **literary agent**, you will need to seek a reputable one which best fits you and your genre. And send them a query letter, outlining what your novel is about, who you are and who your target market is. But even these can be challenging to obtain, so again, prepare for rejection. Agents and publishers are flooded with requests, so it really isn't personal when you get a 'no'. Keep trying!

I'm an **indie author** (self-published) because honestly, I'm a control enthusiast (maybe a freak – LOL). I didn't want someone tearing my book apart, applying their own formula to it, and taking most of the proceeds. If/when I achieve greatness, I want to be able to say, "I made that."

But if you go down the same indie path, then you have the next question… do you want to publish with **Amazon KDP**? Well, as they hold the market share still, then yes, you probably do. However, there is then the question of entering **KDP Select**.

That is the scheme whereby subscribers of Kindle Unlimited can download your ebook for free. You get paid a tiny little bit by page read (KENP). However, this does mean your ebook must be available exclusively to Amazon, not even on offer in giveaways etc. This does not affect any paperbacks, just the ebooks.

My advice on the KDP Select option is to check the Top 100 books in your category. If the majority of those are in Kindle Unlimited, you probably should be too. I know there are authors who disagree with this way of deciding, but you have to use something.

If you decide to "go wide", that is to offer your ebook across many platforms, such as Kobo and Apple Books, there are companies such as Draft2Digital who let you upload your manuscript and push it out to multiple platforms. If you wish to advertise with Amazon (or any others who offer that option), publish with those separately (directly) and ensure you don't select them in your (e.g. Draft2Digital) options.

So, if you've selected self-publishing and Amazon, you will need to create an account on Amazon KDP. And, if you did the 'task' homework in the 'What?" section, you'll already have a good understanding of which **categories** you wish to select.

Amazon KDP no longer allow you to list more than THREE categories, but these are self-selected in KDP when you upload your manuscript. btw Amazon reserve the right to change these. Choose wisely!

Also, if you use KDP Rocket, you may find that some categories listed which duplicate into others automatically (giving you more than the three official ones chosen).

Pricing

Pricing is variable and reliant on genre and length. However, what I will say is that you want to be competitive.

With regards to ebooks, free or 99c for a full-length novel (that's generally a book over 50,000 words), is telling readers you don't value yourself.

But you don't want to ask for too much, either.

$4.99 or $5.99 is now considered the sweet spot at the time of writing this.

Amazon KDP kindly does an easy conversion to the equivalent price for other countries' Amazon sites for you. But check they feel right – they can be manually adjusted.

A quick note on **free books** – in my humble opinion, these are not a good idea. The amount of readers who grab free books in sales is large, granted, but not many go on to read them. And because of the inherent lack of value, even fewer then go on to review freebies. They also tend to promote the notion that authors can afford to give away books without receiving any payment. This is tragically untrue – most authors rely on that money to produce more books.

Having said all that, if the first book in a series is permanently free, that's a bit different. Still not the most comfortable thought, but there is an argument for tempting readers in this way.

Look, I've been around the publishing world for about ten years at this point. I understand the temptation and desperation, really I do. This is my voice of experience. I have witnessed the increasing expectation that all books should be free. But authors have homes and bills just like other people (*sigh*). Readers without sufficient book-purchasing funds should be encouraged to use their local library, if possible – they can even request that your book should be stocked if it isn't already.

Keywords

Keywords in the book's listing are not the same as advertising ones.

As discussed under 'What', Amazon lists things such as 'romantic heroes' and 'romantic themes' under the romance category – these may be good words to use in your keywords e.g. "wealthy", "royalty & aristocrats" or "wedding".

Like the categories, you will need to do a bit of research to discover your best ones. Sites such as Publisher Rocket will help you discover competitive choices.

'Historical romance' is too broad. Drill down into time period, setting, character role, story tone and theme e.g. Renaissance steamy romance, chivalrous knight, arranged marriage or strong female lead.

If you go to the Amazon shopping page, select 'Kindle Books' from the dropdown in the search bar, then start typing a phrase, auto-fill will give you some handy popular search terms. These are also useful when creating Amazon adverts later (*nudge nudge, wink wink*).

You can combine keywords (up to around seven), so try to create a logical phrase e.g. wealthy Regency aristocrat – that would be one 'keyword' option. Or medieval historical fiction.

The aim is to make your book as discoverable as possible.

~ What are the likely words or phrases that readers are going to type in to search for your kind of book?

A good **book description** aka blurb is another absolute must. If that has spelling errors, you've just made a potential reader run for the hills. Also, you need to entice without giving away the entire plot. It's very different from novel writing, so don't sweat it if you find it difficult to do; most of us do. Again, there are resources available to help you. And you'll find my tips in the next section.

Cover – a quick note on book covers; it is seriously worth employing a professional designer to do this for you. It is the first thing potential readers will see, and it will be amidst a plethora of other choices. And, having been in a writing group where authors showed their covers, and others guessed if it was professionally designed... people can tell the difference!

That's the basics of ebook publishing covered. It should be enough to give you a good start.

If you wish to publish a **paperback**, I have an important note for British authors...

If you want even a chance of approaching Waterstones bookshops, you will need a UK distributor, such as Gardners. Amazon does not use these yet. But Ingram Spark does. Just saying.

There are many options for printing too. I mention Ingram Spark as they are a 'print on demand' service under their sister heading of 'Lightning Source' - popular amongst indie authors. Choose who's right for you.

Many considerations come into force, such as trim size and paper colour. If you've used a professional book cover designer, you can send them the printer-supplied template for the correct cover size, and they'll do the complicated stuff.

When pricing paperbacks, your printing company should have a guide to help with that. There is a printing cost which needs to be covered, so pay attention to the royalties they calculate for your book. At the same time, buyers won't want to pay much over £10/$13.

You will also need an ISBN.

For authors in the USA, Bowker is the approved place to purchase these.

For British authors, these are obtained from Nielsen.

Now, confusingly, Nielsen also has a sister site; Nielsen Title Editor, to register the ISBN fully when you have a title and all sorts of metadata so that shops/libraries can see your book. However, Ingram Spark will do this bit for you.

As a British author, by law, you will need to submit a copy of every publication published in the UK to The British Library, even if it's only in electronic format.

You will need to send x5 copies of your paperback to The Agency for the Legal Deposit Libraries, and another to the British Library. There may be certain circumstances when they will solely accept electronic copies, so do check their sites.

Summary of Skills Required (as an Indie Author)

- Writing (creative for the storytelling)
- Copy Edit Writing (for adverts and book description)
- Digital Marketing (including brand management)
- Social Media
- Contract Management (for dealing with editors, cover designers etc.)
- Adaptability (in an ever-changing marketplace)
- Data Analysis (to track your book's/advert performance)
- Bookkeeping (to measure profit/loss)
- Fortitude (to keep going through even the toughest parts)
- Good Sense of Humour (to laugh off any ridiculousness which besets you)

Writing the Book Description

I see so many authors wailing through the book description phase, struggling like mad.

Firstly, this is a very different writing style from novel writing. The 'blurb' is advertising copy, not storytelling.

Secondly, you are not trying to summarise the plot of your book in 200 words. Yeah, read that again! Yes, it should have a maximum of 200 words, but it is not a summary.

The book description needs to give hints of the plot, but without spoilers. It is there to entice a reader to discover more. Think of adverts for other products you see around. This is your version of those.

A stranger is standing in front of you. Tell them what your book is about.

I have seen it said that, following scientific research and broadly speaking, female readers prefer to see a character name in book descriptions whereas male ones don't. Whether you follow this train of thought or not, it is important to think of your target reader.

It's a good idea to look at the top sellers in your category and see how they approach their book descriptions. Would you want to read their book? Why?

There are subtle differences between genres and subgenres. However, in very general terms, here is one approach you can try…

Add **an introductory line** in bold or italics with up to six words – a hook. Set the scene. Then:

- ❖ Start with your main character's emotional state as the book starts.
- ❖ Set the scene for the inciting incident (the big thing).
- ❖ And what is it that changes everything? How does your character feel about that?

Then start a new paragraph.

- ❖ How does your main character react?
- ❖ Hint at the big challenge/hurdle.
- ❖ End on a cliffhanger – what are the stakes (hint; make this as dramatic as possible. It's often a life or death situation tbh).

The main character needs to be seen to take action. What mess are they going to get into? And what might they do about it?

It's also a good idea to try to casually use a couple of keywords. Don't be blatant about it, just drop them in naturally if at all possible.

Read your description a few times. Would you want to read this book?

Then ask some friends and/or other authors you trust. We're often more than willing to help another author, and maybe better at helping others than ourselves – we don't know your story as intimately as our own, so it's easier to detach and get a higher viewpoint.

That being said, authors are very very busy. If you ask and we politely say no, please don't be upset – it's nothing personal.

Trigger Warnings

I see a lot of authors panicking about these. Trigger warnings should be considered when writing a book description. Be upfront, put them at the bottom of your description if required.

Here's my perspective as a trained counsellor:

Firstly, there are two different types of triggers.

Emotional Triggers

Someone may make a joke, but to you it hurts and can affect you, making you feel off-kilter. You question whether the person making the joke respects you or not.

Feelings brought up can include:

- ❖ A sense of rejection
- ❖ Being left/singled out
- ❖ Disapproval

~ basically, you feel inferior in some way

Reactions to this can include:

- ❖ Withdrawal
- ❖ Anger
- ❖ Self-medication (drugs/alcohol/food etc.)
- ❖ Compliance

These are normal human reactions and are often associated with things from your own past. It is your reaction based on previous experience, and not the fault of the person making the joke, which to everyone else is harmless.

This does not mean in any way that it is your fault either. It's just one of those less pleasant experiences of life. The good news is, there are coping mechanisms and people trained to help you with this.

Emotional triggers are **not** what trigger warnings are about, as we cannot feasibly foresee how every single person is going to react. We all have the potential to associate an infinite number of innocuous things with a negative reaction.

Psychological Triggers

These go way beyond our feelings being trampled on (which is unpleasant enough, right?). They are so much more.

These types of triggers can be set off with a particular sound, smell or sight which are associated with trauma and often cause flashbacks. Often used in conjunction with PTSD (and other anxiety conditions), and commonly (but not exclusively) include post-war/combat soldiers and survivors of sexual abuse.

Flashbacks are no laughing matter. They have oddly become more common since movies started. And it is a bit like watching a film, only this is the 3D, fully immersive version. Your brain throws you right back into the traumatic event, and you relive it as if you were there again. It is terrifying, debilitating and to be avoided. It is deeply traumatic in itself.

These are the folk we need/want to protect.

We do not want to drive anyone to despair.

In all fairness to them, a little word of caution so there are no nasty surprises is a simple courtesy which can save severe pain and suffering.

It serves as a warning for survivors to put their coping strategies in place and/or choose not to read a book they will find too difficult to cope with.

By the way, they may well choose to read your book anyway. With the correct coping strategies in place, it may help them face/overcome their issue/s.

What we are doing is offering them the information so they may make an informed decision.

Trigger warnings give people the power of control and choice.

So, if your book (especially if it's unexpected) contains scenes of:

- Violence/war
- Sexual/physical/mental abuse
- Mental illness
- Oppressive/hateful language or behaviour
- Self-harm
- Eating disorders
- Death/suicide
- Pregnancy/miscarriage/abortion

...please put a trigger warning under the book description to save long-term psychological damage.

It just makes sense, doesn't it?

And, if warnings *are* necessary, it's a nice idea to include helplines in your back matter.

To help you further, the dictionary definition of trauma:

Trauma   /ˈtrɔːmə,ˈtraʊmə/   noun
~ A deeply distressing or disturbing experience.
"*a personal trauma like the death of a child*"

~ Mass noun; emotional shock following a stressful event or a physical injury, which may lead to long-term neurosis.
'*the event is relived with all the accompanying trauma*'

Basically, events outside the ordinary, expected human experience. Or experience which involves actual or threatened death or severe injury (of self or others). Involves overwhelming fear, helplessness and/or horror.

This information is meant to inform and educate, not to criticise or belittle.

My aim is to help authors decide whether or not to include a trigger warning under their book description, and the reasons why.

And to bring a little perspective to the confusion that exists out there.

OK, on to happier thoughts.

Reviews

Firstly; *never ever* pay for reviews. Possibly maybe with the exception of Kirkus book reviews, but they are really expensive and may not even be favourable – you choose whether it's worth it for you or not.

Reviews are ever so helpful, though. They help let other readers know if a book's worthy of their purchase. But also, as I'll mention under 'Advertising', they may help you get a high-value ad spot. The more reviews the better!

Sadly, the statistics for 'organic' reviews are low – around 85% of readers do NOT review books. It's estimated only *one out of two thousand readers* actually do write a review! This was deeply shocking to me, as I've always left reviews, even before I became an author.

Amazon does not like friends or family leaving reviews. Given mine are my harshest critics, I fail to see why. However, some people are blessed with overly kind relatives, I suppose. Amazon goes through regularly, deleting reviews from people who look like SPAM or if they have a vague connection with yourself; sadly, it never seems to be the 1* trolls who get wiped off. But hey ho.

Running giveaways rarely results in such things either, in my experience. Very mean-spirited, if you ask me.

So, how *do* you get reviews? Well, one thing I've not mentioned yet is the importance of building an ARC team. You can seek beta readers (people who check an early draft for things such as plot holes) and/or ARC (Advanced Reader Copy) readers in places such as Facebook. Or put a plea out on social media. Just make sure you trust them – there are scammy pirates out there. I try to check their presence on Goodreads to verify their track record for reviewing.

Some websites gather book reviewer information very nicely e.g. The Indie View - you can filter for those who review indie authors and your genre. These should be FREE reviews! Each person will have their way of submitting your book for review – either via their website or email; follow their instructions closely!

Do note that popular book bloggers are in high demand. If they're even accepting submissions, you may want to give them around two months' notice.

The ones who a) accept and then b) actually review are rare treasures. **Keep a log** of their names and contact details, so you can ask them again when you have another book out. They are more likely to say yes once they know they like your style.

This is a slow process, so make some time to go through it thoroughly.

Advertising

So, if you've got through all of that and pressed that big, scary "publish" button, then give yourself a big cheer, pat on the back and maybe a celebratory drink of your choosing. You did it – that thing which so many say they want to do but have never had the courage to actually do. You have now reached lion/ess status of bravery.

However, what you thought was the end of your author journey turns out to be merely a beginning. For now, you must tell others that your book exists. I hate to be the one to break it to you, but there are millions of other books listed, and sadly, readers won't magically know yours is there. I know, right? Eurgh! Rude! So, you need to advertise.

THERE IS NO ONE WAY WHICH WORKS FOR EVERYONE!

Just saying as there are so many opinions on advertising and marketing. What works for some doesn't work for others, so there will be an element of trial and error.

Having a **social media** presence is a good, solid recommendation. Find where your target market hangs out, and sign up there. You can start with one e.g. Instagram, and work your way up. However, social media is not really there for advertising. It is about building connections. There are wonderful writing communities online, and when you find the right ones, it's a fab place of like-minded, supportive souls.

When posting on social media, you will want some excellent **teaser images**. You can create these fairly easily yourself. Grab some quality, royalty-free, stock images from a site such as Deposit Photos (this is a paid subscription, but there are sometimes deals to be had). It's worth paying for these from reputable sites so you don't get into trouble.

Feel free to take your own book photos too btw.

You can then get onto a graphic design site, such as Canva (paid and free options available) to get creative.

You can use review quotes or quotes from your book. Maybe do a mood board image. Create a presentation for IG Reels/TikTok. Talking of which, why not read a little excerpt of your book in a video? There are so many options. Have a play.

Marketing gurus suggest having your own website too. I have a blog site, where I share writing tips, book reviews for others and random things. It is also the place you can sign up to my **newsletter**. This is also a highly useful thing to have.

Authors seem to use Mailchimp or MailerLite to send their newsletters. They are basically your hosts for those.

And there are newsletter builder sites, such as Prolific Works or Booksprout, so you can start building your subscribers. You will need at least a snippet or short story to take part in these, as you give those away as a 'magnet' for signups – make sure it's not your Kindle Unlimited book for this though!

Your newsletter frequency is up to you. I send one per month with details on my progress and also book news of other authors. Most authors I see tend to have this frequency. Again, it's a personal choice.

In terms of pure advertising, my biggest hitter is **BookBub**. There are those who claim great success with their self-serve ads, and many who don't. The thing you want to aim for is their **Featured Deal**, maybe on a 99c sale instead of a free book. You will want lots of reviews first, though. They have a criterion for allowing one of these, and with good reason. Featured Deals are expensive and have an upfront cost! They want you to get your money's worth, and it's their reputation on the line too. So, if you don't get one on your first try, keep trying each month – my first took over twenty attempts to get accepted!

They have millions of subscribers, and I've always at least made my money back. And Regency Love reached "bestseller" status on multiple Amazon sites with a BookBub Featured Deal on a 99c sale. Although, this is not guaranteed - it is always a gamble.

The other advertising method I suggest is Amazon's own (**AMS**). But, you need to learn to do it properly. There are free courses such as those run by The Kindlepreneur, and Bryan Cohen – I've done both of these and found them immensely helpful. At the end of the day, most of your readers will be on Amazon searching for books, so it's a good idea to push your book onto their radar, right?

With AMS, you only pay for the adverts potential readers *click* on. So, it's a lower upfront cost. The trick is to convert those clicks into sales and turn a profit, hence the course recommendations. This is also part of the reason for needing an awesome cover and blurb.

Online Presence

I already briefly mentioned social media but thought it worthy of its own section with further explanation.

Before you even launch your book, it's a good idea to start a social media following. Instagram is my personal go-to as there is a great writing community there. It's not necessarily to sell books but to mingle and give/receive support.

TikTok is increasingly popular. But you still have the options of Facebook and Twitter. Follow accounts that share your bookish interests, so the algorithm is appeased.

And don't forget to have a website and newsletter.

There are so many options, and it can be daunting. You don't have to show your face – you can just show things like page flips, where you film flicking through your book then overlaying text or speech excerpts. Or get lots of images which represent your book's aesthetic.

Social media is the place where readers will get to know you. Don't be all "buy my book". Include some things, such as pictures of your writing space/process, book buddies (pets) and/or places of interest that you visit/research.

You will need a nice **profile photo**. Ideally, this will be the same on each platform so readers can easily identify you as they hop around the internet. They tend to be a tight-cropped, head and shoulders shot.

You may want to reflect your genre in your attire, and also portray your personality a little too. As we're focusing on historical fiction here, maybe you want old brickwork or a monument in the background (be careful it doesn't look like it's on top of your head or shoulder though!).

Your facial expression is also important. And lighting shouldn't be ignored. Take a look at other comparable authors to yourself and get inspired. I'm not going to say look at mine; it's side-on, for a start, which isn't usually advised. I'm just quirky.

An **author bio** is a very handy thing to keep in your press toolkit folder – you will use it in many places. Basically, every time you set up an author page.

An author bio aims to give readers some information about you as an author to help them gain trust in your credibility/talent. And it should be written in the third person.

The first sentence should be something short and snappy – a 'hook'. After all, some people may not read past that. What is it you do? What experience do you have? And have you got any accolades?

Mine starts: *TL Clark is a best-selling, award-winning, British, romance author who stumbles through life as if it were a gauntlet of catastrophes.*

Then you can fill in some relevant biographical details – a hint of your 'why' and maybe mention any books you've written already. Feel free to add a flare of your personality. But keep it under 300 words.

Mine ends: *Rather than playing the victim, she uses these unfortunate events to fuel her passion for writing, for reaching out to help others.*

She writes about different kinds of love in the hope that she'll uncover its mysteries.

Her loving husband (and very spoiled cat) have proven to her that true love really does exist.

Writing has shown her that coffee may well be the source of life.

There is an Author Page on Amazon. This isn't obvious, as you set it up via www.author.amazon.com.

This will need to be done for each "marketplace" e.g. US and UK.

It houses all your books and your bio. You can also include feeds from other social media.

Other good places to have an author page/account include Goodreads and BookBub. You should review other books on these sites too a) because it's nice and you want to be supportive and b) because it will help boost your visibility.

Press Toolkit

So, in a folder on your computer, it's a good idea to have some things handy for when you're approaching the media, or even just general social media interaction. Things to include are:

- ❖ Author profile pic (this should ideally be the same everywhere)
- ❖ Author bio
- ❖ Press release
- ❖ Book description/tagline info
- ❖ A document for your links (e.g. author pages/book links)
- ❖ Tracker for any guest blogs or interviews you've done

By the way, a really handy link to use is something like a **Universal Book Link** which can be done via www.books2read.com (accessed via Draft2Digital). This sets up one link which will take your readers to their preferred store in their country. One link to rule them all!

You may or may not decide to write a **press release**. Some people rave about them. It's basically a brief document highlighting the main points why journalists want to write about your book.

There are vast numbers of books published all the time (millions each year), and most large media outlets won't want to cover indie authors. Hence my reticence on this requirement.

If you decide to go for this option, your book needs to be relevant/newsworthy. Does it tie in with current events or social media trends? Was it inspired by some life-changing moment that will give others hope?

The press release should be written in the third person and have an attention-grabbing headline. Include the date and your city – especially important for local press.

Show the journalist why your book is important. And give them a synopsis. Include a short quote. And don't forget your author bio and contact details.

This is merely information to get you thinking about whether you want/need to have a press release and generally what its aim is.

Checklist for Self-Publishing

- ☐ Write a great book!
- ☐ Ensure it's well-edited
- ☐ Write a captivating blurb
- ☐ Select a launch date
- ☐ Create a launch strategy
- ☐ For paperbacks: obtain your ISBN
- ☐ Get an awesome cover

~ for paperbacks; first, get the template from your printers to ensure the correct size

- ☐ Upload your ebook and paperback files to your chosen companies e.g. Amazon KDP or Ingram Spark
- ☐ Approach ARC readers
- ☐ Contact the distributor e.g. Gardners to ensure your book is available
- ☐ Check on/contact stores such as Waterstones or WH Smith to ensure your book is available on their site
- ☐ Ensure your book appears on Goodreads (ask their librarians if not)
- ☐ Ensure your book appears on BookBub
- ☐ Ensure your book displays correctly on Amazon etc.

~ your paperback and ebook should appear on the same page
~ contact KDP Help if they do not merge within 72hrs

- ☐ Approach any advertisers/media with your launch campaign/press release
- ☐ Do a cover reveal
- ☐ Create many promotional pics/videos/blog posts

- ☐ Update your book page on your own website/social media pinned posts
- ☐ Set up pre-order advertising
- ☐ Set up launch day promo
- ☐ Send paperback copies to Agency for the Legal Deposit Libraries, and the British Library (as appropriate)
- ☐ Set up longer-term ads, such as AMS (Amazon)
- ☐ LAUNCH! Celebrate here!!
- ☐ Track ARC reviewers who have left reviews
- ☐ Keep promoting

NB At every stage, remember to breathe! You got this.

- ☐ Then repeat – yes, keep writing. Your chances of success grow with each book.

Final Thoughts

Remember at the beginning of this book, under "Why?", I said '*Write because you love it*'? Maybe you have glimpsed into that why now?

Yes, all of this probably sounds complicated and daunting. Writing and self-publishing take dedication. It's hard work. And there's a steep learning curve. But when you get people from across the globe purchasing your 'book baby', it's the best feeling in the world!

Writing should be a pleasurable experience. Yes, there are tribulations, but the good should outweigh the bad. We share our stories with the world because we have that inner drive to do so.

Hopefully, this book has helped set out enough of the basics to pave the way for you. It contains a lot of information I wish I'd known before I started. It is intended to help, not put you off, whilst also managing expectations.

Please allow me to issue my thanks to you for reading this book. I truly hope you now go on to write a wonderful historical novel and publish it. Feel free to let me know if/when you do. My contact details are in the 'About the Author' section at the end of this book.

Of course, if you did find all of this information helpful, please also feel free to leave a review – you now know how much they're valued (*flutters eyelashes*).

Useful Websites

- ❖ Grammarly (spelling/grammar checker): www.grammarly.com
- ❖ Reedsy (a great source of writing advice/resources): reedsy.com
- ❖ BISG (for BISAC subject codes): bisg.org

- ❖ ISBN (for USA authors): www.bowker.com
- ❖ ISBN (for British author purchasing): www.nielsenisbnstore.com
- ❖ ISBN (for British author registration): www.nielsentitleeditor.com/titleeditor

- ❖ The Agency for the Legal Deposit Libraries: www.legaldeposit.org.uk
- ❖ The British Library (to register your claim on reading royalties): www.bl.uk/plr

- ❖ Gardners (UK distributor): www.gardners.com/Selling-To-Us

- ❖ Deposit Photos (royalty-free stock images): www.depositphotos.com
- ❖ Canva (to design teasers): www.canva.com

- ❖ The Indie View (for reviewer info): www.theindieview.com/indie-reviewers

- ❖ BookBub (for Featured Deal ads & leaving reviews): www.bookbub.com/launch

- ❖ Goodreads (ensure your book is listed & leave reviews for others): www.goodreads.com

- ❖ Universal Book Link (Books2Read): www.books2read.com

- ❖ Ingram Spark (paperback print-on-demand): www.ingramspark.com

Amazon:
- ❖ KDP (to set up book etc.): www.kdp.amazon.com
- ❖ Author page setup/management: www.author.amazon.com/home
- ❖ AMS advertising: www.advertising.amazon.com

- ❖ Prolific Works (newsletter builder): www.prolificworks.com
- ❖ Booksprout (alternative newsletter builder): wwww.booksprout.co

Courses:
- ❖ Kindlepreneur: www.courses.kindlepreneur.com/courses
- ❖ Bryan Cohen: www.facebook.com/bryan.cohen.50

My blog: www.tlclarkauthor.blogspot.com
'Search' for articles such as:
- ❖ Indie author vs Traditional Publishing
- ❖ Kindle Unlimited vs Wide
- ❖ How to Beat Writer's Block
- ❖ Regency research posts
- ❖ 15th century (medieval) research

About the Author

TL Clark is an award-winning, best-selling, British author of love who stumbles through life as if it were a gauntlet of catastrophes. Rather than playing the victim, she uses these unfortunate events to fuel her passion for writing, for reaching out to help others.

She writes about different kinds of love in the hope that she'll uncover its mysteries. This has led to her hopping around the romance subgenres like a loved-up froggy.

Her dream is to buy a farmhouse, so she can run a retreat for those who are feeling frazzled by the stresses of the modern world. And to run writing retreats – authors are some of the most frazzled humans anyway.

Her loving husband (and mourned-for cat) have proven to her that true love really does exist.
Writing has shown her that coffee may well be the source of life.

If you would like to follow TL on social media, @tlclarkauthor will usually find her. She is most usually to be found on **Instagram** or **TikTok**.

Or simply scan this handy QR code to sign up to her newsletter:

Novels by TL Clark
You're Most Likely to Enjoy

Love Habit – A positive LGBTQIA+ historical tale of two novice monks. Set in 15th century England.

Love in the Roses – Isabel is the daughter of a knight and is about to marry a man she's never met. Also set in 15th century England.

Regency Love – Discover what Lady Anne really thinks as she enters the marriage mart in 1814.

A Haverton Christmas - A short story spin-off of Regency Love. Lady Caroline returns empty-handed from the Season, and her Christmas looks bleak.

Miss Georgiana Darcy's Quest For Love – A Pride & Prejudice variation novelette. Discover what happened to Georgiana after her dealings with Mr Wickham.

But should you wish to diversify your reading, please note she also has contemporary, inspirational and fantasy romance options available.

www.ingramcontent.com/pod-product-compliance
Lightning Source LLC
Chambersburg PA
CBHW070601010526
44118CB00012B/1415